Office Practice Dictionary

M Steer

D1808390

Pitman

PITMAN PUBLISHING LIMITED
128 Long Acre, London WC2E 9AN

Associated Companies
Pitman Publishing Pty Ltd, Melbourne
Pitman Publishing New Zealand Ltd, Wellington

© M Steer 1985

First published in Great Britain 1985

British Library Cataloguing in Publication Data
Steer, M.
  Office practice dictionary.
  1. Office practice
  I. Title
  651   HF5547.5

Typeset in 10/12 pt Palatino and printed in Great Britain
at The Pitman Press, Bath

ISBN 0 273 02258 X

Topics covered include

Abbreviations (*These appear at the head of each letter in the Dictionary*)
Applications for Employment
British Telecom Services
Business Documents
Business Organisation
Business Organisations
Clearing Bank Services
Communications
Computers
Correction Signs
Filing and Indexing
Girobank Services
Health and Safety at Work
Income Tax
Mailing Room
Meetings
Methods of Payment
National Insurance
Office Machinery and Equipment
Office Stationery
Office Stock
Petty Cash
Post Office Services and Post Office Savings
Reception Duties
Reprographics
Royal Mail Services
Salaries and Wages
Sources of Information
Telephone Alphabet (*This appears at the head of each letter in the Dictionary*)
Transactions
Word Processors

Acknowledgments

The author and publishers would like to thank the following for supplying material for reproduction in this book:

Banking Information Service: figs 5, 6, 10, 11, 12, 13, 54
Barclays Bank plc: fig 4
British Telecommunications: figs 48, 57
The Controller, Her Majesty's Stationery Office: figs 31, 32, 33, 34
Midland Bank plc: fig 19
National Girobank: figs 24, 25, 26, 27, 28, 29
National Westminster Bank: fig 14
Pitney-Bowes: figs 1, 20, 23, 30, 37, 39, 53
Rank Xerox (UK) Limited: figs 18, 41, 45, 59
Royal Mail (The Post Office): figs 15, 49, 50
The Times
Universal Postal Union, Berne, Switzerland: fig 52

A

Abbreviations

@	at
AA	Automobile Association
A/C or a/c	account
ADC	advice of duration and charge
advt.	advertisement
AGM	annual general meeting
amt	amount
AOB	any other business
ASP.	accelerated surface post
assn.	association

Absent card/absent folder (filing) Also known as an **outcard/out folder**. If a file has been borrowed from a filing system an absent card should be put in its place until its return. It should record:
1 The name or number of the file.
2 The name, department and extension number of the borrower.
3 The date it was borrowed.
An absent card should be the same size as the file it replaces, and should remain in place until the file is returned and the entry on the card cancelled.

Absentee One who is absent from the place where he is normally expected to be.

Accelerated Surface Post (ASP) (Royal Mail International) A contract service for those posting large volumes of printed paper.

Account rendered (a/c rendered) (business documents) The opening entry on a Statement of Account which shows any balance which was outstanding at the beginning of the period covered. It is usually an amount which has appeared on a previous statement but which has not been paid.

Accounts Department The Chief Accountant is responsible for all the financial records of a firm; he must be able to show at any time its present financial position and what he anticipates the position will be in the future. He will be expected to advise management on all matters concerning finance and is responsible for the preparation of the annual accounts.

The *Cashier's Department* is a sub-division of the Accounts Department and is concerned with all transactions involving cash.

The Cashier works closely with the *Salaries and Wages Department* which calculates the earnings of all employees.

A *Junior Accounts Clerk* should be good at figures and able to produce neatly written work. Like all other junior staff she should be courteous, pleasant, friendly and helpful at all times.

Accrue To accumulate and add to.

Acknowledgment, acknowledgment card/slip These were used widely in the past but increasing postal costs have forced economies in their usage.

It is still necessary to send an acknowledgment if the reply to a letter is unavoidably delayed; some firms send acknowledgments of orders especially if the delivery date is not immediate.

Acknowledgments are usually form letters (qv) printed on postcards, where only the addressee's name and address and a minimal amount of information are to be inserted.

Acoustic hood (word processors) A box that covers a printer and deadens some of the noise it makes.

Acronym A word formed from the first letters, or first few letters, of several other words. ERNIE (premium bonds) is an acronym for Electronic Random Number Indicator Equipment.

Adding/listing machines These machines add and subtract, and each machine is provided with a tally roll on which calculations are printed.

Addressee The person (or firm) to whom a communication is addressed.

Addressing machines/labellers (outgoing mail) See fig 1.

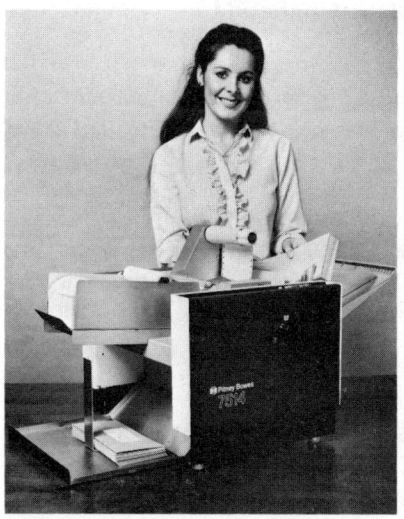

Fig 1 Addressing machine/labeller

Addressing mail

Metal stencils or embossed metal plates are made to order, each bearing one name and address. These, together with envelopes or adhesive address labels are fed into the machine and the addresses printed.

Word processors are also used for addressing large quantities of circulars, accounts, etc, and have the advantage that changes to the lists can be effected easily. They also print names and addresses on labels, or directly onto envelopes, statements or circulars, as required.

Electronic addressing systems are controlled by a microprocessor and the information is held on mini diskettes. New addresses, deletions and amendments are entered by a typewriter-style keyboard and are displayed on a VDU. Labels can then be addressed automatically at a speed of up to 9000 per hour.

Addressing mail (outgoing mail) See fig 2. All mail should be clearly and properly addressed. The postcode should always be the last item in the address, and on a line by itself.

Ad hoc (meetings) These Latin words mean 'for this special purpose'. An ad hoc meeting is one called for a particular purpose.

Advice note (business documents) Also known as a **despatch note**. This tells the customer that his goods are being despatched from the warehouse or factory, and the method by which they are to be transported.

Advice of Duration and Charge (ADC) (British Telecom) In order to discover the duration and charge of a telephone call the caller should ask the operator for ADC at the time the call is booked. ADC calls cannot be dialled direct. The number to ring for the ADC service is shown in the preface of the local telephone directory.

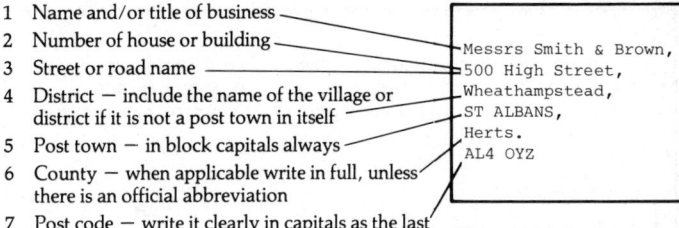

1. Name and/or title of business
2. Number of house or building
3. Street or road name
4. District — include the name of the village or district if it is not a post town in itself
5. Post town — in block capitals always
6. County — when applicable write in full, unless there is an official abbreviation
7. Post code — write it clearly in capitals as the last line of the address

```
Messrs Smith & Brown,
500 High Street,
Wheathampstead,
ST ALBANS,
Herts.
AL4 OYZ
```

This example has been typed with *full* punctuation.

```
Messrs Smith & Brown
500 High Street
Wheathampstead
ST ALBANS
Herts
AL4 OYZ
```

This example has been typed with *open* punctuation — there are no commas or stops at the ends of the lines.

Fig 2 Addressing mail

Aerogramme (Royal Mail) This may be sent to any address in the world. It must not contain enclosures and must be written either on the stamped forms which are obtainable from post offices or on privately manufactured forms for which the postage must be prepaid.

Agenda (meetings)   See fig 3. A list of items drawn up by the Chairman and sent out by the Secretary, which are to be discussed at a meeting in the order in which they are shown.
The agenda should be distributed *before* the meeting to the committee members, and extra copies should be available at the meeting itself.

```
A MEETING OF THE EXECUTIVE COMMITTEE OF THE EASTLAKE
COMMUNITY ASSOCIATION WILL BE HELD IN THE VILLAGE HALL
(ROOM 2) IN MAIN STREET, EASTLAKE, ON FRIDAY 2 SEPTEMBER
19.. AT 7.30 PM

A G E N D A

* 1   Apologies for absence
* 2   Minutes of the last meeting
* 3   Business arising out of the minutes (Matters arising)
  4   Treasurer's financial statement
  5   Report on donations received
  6   To consider the establishment of a Sports Club
  7   To consider life membership of the Association
* 8   Any other business (AOB)
* 9   Date and time of the next meeting

NAOMI HONITON

Secretary
```

*Items 1, 2, 3, 8 and 9 must appear on *every* agenda

Fig 3 Agenda

Airmail (Royal Mail) Letters (including letter packets) and postcards *for Europe* are sent by air as the normal means of transmission whenever this will result in earlier postal delivery. This is known as the **all-up service**. There is no special charge for air conveyance and no special need for airmail marking.

For other overseas air mail the charge is greater than that for surface mail, and blue air mail labels must be positioned close to the addresses on all letters, packets and parcels.

Airway letters (Royal Mail) By agreement with the Post Office, British Airways accept first class letters from the public at certain airport offices and convey them on the next available direct air service to the destination, to be called for at the airport or transferred to the ordinary post by the airline. An additional fee is payable to the airline for each airway letter.

Alarm call (British Telecom)   To be awakened early in the morning a subscriber may ask the operator to telephone at a specific time. Alarm calls should be booked, preferably, before 10.30 pm the previous evening. There is a charge for this service.

Algorithm (computers)   The procedural steps for the solution of a specific problem. A simple example is a food recipe.

All-up service (Royal Mail)   Letters (including letter packets) and postcards *for Europe* are sent by air as the normal means of transmission whenever this will result in earlier postal delivery. This is known as the all-up service: there is no special charge for air conveyance and no special need for airmail marking.

Alphabetical filing   One of the five main filing systems where papers are filed in the order of the letters of the alphabet.
The following hints are taken from the preface of a local Telephone Directory, and are reproduced by the kind permission of British Telecommunications plc:
1   Surnames are in alphabetical order.
   Brodie
   Brogan
   Brooks
   Brough
2   Entries with the same surname are in alphabetical order of initials.
   Brown A
   Brown A A

> Brown A C
> Brown A C A
> Brown A C B
> Brown A D

The position of entries which include forenames is decided only by the initials.

> Brown Andrew D
> Brown Alex E
> Brown A F

3   Entries consisting wholly or partly of initials are listed before surnames beginning with the same initial letter:

> ABK (Bakers) Ltd   is listed *before*
> Aabcon A

4   Apostrophes and hyphens—a name such as Hall-Smith is sorted as though the hyphen were not present and it were written Hallsmith. Apostrophes are similarly disregarded.

5   Prefixes—surnames or titles beginning with the abbreviation 'St' are listed after 'Saint'. The prefixes 'M', 'Mc' and 'Mac' are all treated as 'Mac' and the next letter in the name determines the position on the list.

6   Names starting with a separate prefix such as 'De', 'Du', 'La', 'Le', 'Van', etc, are sorted so that all the names with the same prefix come together and the order between them is then determined by the second word in the name. Thus Le Blanc comes in front of Le Brun, but both entries come in front of Lea.

7   Numeric entries—numeric entries, eg 123 Social Club, are listed before all alphabetical entries.

Add to these four further rules:

8   Ignore all titles—Dr John Smith would be filed under John Smith and would be written Smith, Dr John.

9   Ignore 'The' and 'Co' when filing names of companies.

10   File government departments under the key word—

the Department of the Environment would be filed under Environment, Department of.

11   A good general rule is that 'nothing' comes before 'something.' A surname alone come before a surname with an initial; and a surname with one initial comes before a surname with two initials:

Smith
Smith J
Smith J J

Alphabetical index   This is composed of a number of record cards on which the first entry will be the name of the person or firm to whom it refers. Beneath this will be shown all the relevant information required by users of the index. Whenever numerical filing is used there must be an alphabetical card index of the names or subjects giving the associated number so that by using the cross-reference a file can be located when only the name is known.

Alphanumeric (word processors)   A type of field within a record that can hold letters or numbers. Also describes a character that can be either a numeral or a letter of the alphabet.

Analysis columns (petty cash)   When heading analysis columns for the Petty Cash Account some or all of the following are used: Postage, Cleaning, Stationery, Travelling Expenses, Office Expenses, Sundries.

Annual General Meeting (AGM)   Yearly meeting which all members of a club, association or society are entitled to attend. The officers and committee for the year are elected at this meeting.

Annual inventory (office stock)   This is the *Annual Stock Count* which involves stocktaking of furniture, equipment, fixtures and fittings and is usually made in addition to the annual stocktaking of items in the stockrooms. It is needed for accounting purposes, and the information is also useful when it comes to assessing the amount of insurance cover needed by the firm against fire and theft.

Answer-back code (Telex) When a Telex operator dials another subscriber's Telex number, the correspondent's answerback code (an abbreviated name) must appear on the teleprinter before any further action can be taken. When it appears the operator types his or her own answer-back code followed by the message.

Answering machines and **Answering/recording machines** (British Telecom) These machines 'answer' the telephone when the subscriber is out or busy. The machine makes an announcement which can be changed as often as required, advising the caller as to when and where the subscriber can be contacted.

Answering/recording machines not only answer the telephone but invite callers to leave a message. These machines can be used to take orders, the number to ring in such cases often being a Freefone number.

Anti-trap envelopes These have double flaps which prevent smaller items being entrapped when the envelope is sent unsealed.

Any other business (AOB) (meetings) Item which must appear on every agenda after details of all known subjects for discussion have been listed. It allows an opportunity for urgent matters which have arisen and cannot wait until the next meeting to be brought forward. See **Agenda**—fig 3.

Aperture cards (microfilming) These are punched cards with a single microfilm and are suitable for plans, drawings, etc.

Aperture envelopes These have cut-out panels through which the address written on the letter can be read.

Apologies for absence (meetings) Item which must appear on every agenda. Committee members who are unable to attend a meeting should notify the Secretary beforehand, so that their non-attendance can be announced to those present at the meeting and recorded in the minutes. See **Agenda**—fig 3.

Application for a post When applying for a post great care should be taken in writing the letter of application and in the preparation of a *curriculum vitae*. Details of both are given under their own headings.

Appointments The most usual form of diary for executives and their secretaries is the 'page-a-day' desk diary, which may be obtained with half- or quarter-hour times already printed for entering the times of business appointments. It is essential that an entry is made for every appointment or interview arranged. Form letters are useful for sending the times and dates of appointments.

Appointments book This is the business diary (qv) in which all appointments and interviews are recorded in advance.

Asterisk A reference mark resembling a star (*).

Attention line (business letters) If letters are to be addressed to the company and not to individuals the name of the person who is to deal with the letter is typed between the address and salutation on the letter itself, thus: FOR THE ATTENTION OF MR A SMITH.

Audio-typist Typist able to type directly on to the machine material reproduced by a dictating machine through earphones or a speaker.
The audio-typist must not only be an accurate typist, but should have a good command of the English language, and be able to spell and punctuate, and correct any errors

in the recording. She will often work in a typing pool where a centralised recording unit will record dictation from executives who are some distance away. The work received is shared out by the supervisor among the audio-typists.

Personal secretaries will have individual transcribing machines for use with tapes dictated by their own executives.

Automatic repeat (electronic typewriters/word processors) A feature of certain electronic keyboards in which a character is automatically repeated if its key is held down.

B

In the Telephone Alphabet B is for Benjamin

Abbreviations

bal	balance
BBC	British Broadcasting Corporation
B/E	bill of exchange
b/f	brought forward
B/L	bill of lading
bn	been
BR	British Rail
bros	brothers
BRS	British Road Services
BST	British Summer Time
BTI	British Telecom International

Background (word processors)   A part of a word processor that takes care of work not needing attention. For example, printing can be done in background leaving the operator free to enter or edit text.

Backing store (computer hardware)   Data or programs currently stored in the memory can be transferred to disks or tapes separate from the computer.

Backspace (word processors)   A key which, when pressed, makes the cursor move one position to the left. This key is used to correct simple typing mistakes on the line of text.

Bank/Banking   There are four main commercial banks in the United Kingdom: Barclays, Lloyds, Midland, National Westminster (NatWest). They are also known as *clearing* or *joint-stock* banks.

The function of these 'High Street' Banks is—

1   To accept deposits.

2   To act as agents for payment (by means of cheques, direct debits, credit transfers, standing orders).

3   To safeguard the money deposited with them, and to lend it to customers (by loans and overdrafts).

Bank customers may hold different types of account. For details of these and the services offered see **Current account, Deposit account, Savings account, Joint account** and **Budget account**.

Some banking services are offered to non-account holders. Among these are the supply of foreign currency and traveller's cheques, banker's credit cards and safe deposit facilities.

The national banking system operated from the post offices and offering a competitive service to that of the clearing banks is known as *Girobank*. Girobank customers may also avail themselves of current, deposit and budget account facilities.

Banker envelopes (stationery)   These are envelopes with the opening on the longer side.

Banker's credit card   See fig 4. A method of payment through the Clearing Banks. Access Cards are issued jointly by Lloyds, Midland and NatWest Banks; Barclaycard by Barclays Bank.

These cards enable the holder to buy goods or services at any shop, restaurant, garage, etc, which has joined the scheme, without paying by cash or cheque at the time of making the purchase. Each shop in the scheme is allotted a 'floor limit' beyond which it cannot accept a credit card in payment for goods without first confirming the transaction by telephone with the credit card company. Also each card holder is given an overall personal limit which cannot be exceeded.

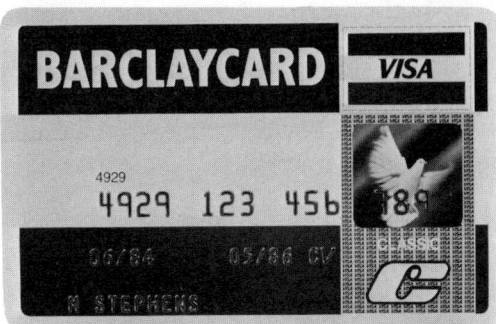

Fig 4 Banker's credit card

The card is presented and a voucher is signed by the card holder. The supplier sends one copy of the voucher to the credit card company by paying it into his bank account. The card holder retains the original voucher for his records and is presented with a statement at the end of the month showing all the transactions he has made with the card during that month. This account he settles by one monthly payment, thereby saving the necessity of carrying cash around and reducing the number of entries on his bank account and possibly also his bank charges; the account can be paid in full or by instalments at which stage interest will be charged. There are many thousands of shops, garages, restaurants and other places which belong to the scheme and it is possible to do a great part of one's spending in this way. It is however important to keep some record and to use the card with discretion.

The card will also enable the holder to obtain cash up to a given limit at any of the branches within the issuing bank's system.

Banker's draft

Banks will issue credit cards to persons who do not hold a current account with them.

Banker's Credit Cards may be used when travelling abroad. The sales voucher is signed in the normal way and shows the cost in the local currency. The transaction appears on the card holder's statement showing the sterling equivalent.

Banker's draft   A method of payment through the Clearing Banks or Girobank. It is, in effect, a cheque drawn on the bank itself.

It is used if businesses are uncertain of the credit-worthiness of persons or firms who owe them money. They may then insist on payment being by means of a banker's draft, rather than by the normal cheque. This means that the firm which owes the money will pay its bank the amount it owes, and the bank will then make out a cheque drawn on itself and made payable to the creditor. This type of cheque is known as a banker's draft.

Banker's (standing) order   See **Standing order**.

Bank giro credit slip (current account)   See fig 5: Method of payment through the Clearing Banks. For single items

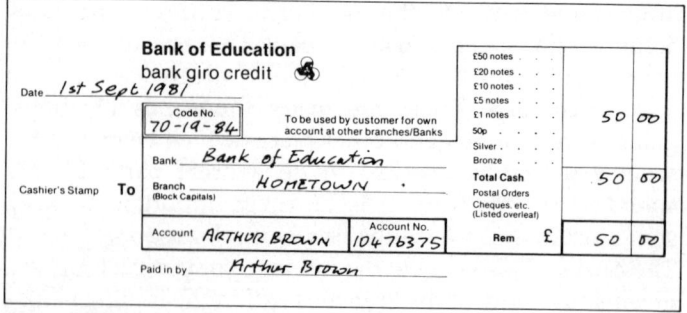

Fig 5 Bank giro credit slip

the bank giro credit provides a convenient and economical means of paying money through the banking system and can be used by both customer and non-customer. It saves the inconvenience of obtaining money orders or postal orders and sending a letter.

The system may be used for settling accounts, such as gas or electricity bills, or for paying into a bank account when away from home. In the latter case the account-holder will write the name and address of the bank where his account is kept; the bank receiving the money will send it to its head office, who will pass it on to the correct bank branch where the account is to be credited.

By means of the bank giro Credit Transfer Schedule a customer is able to have any number of amounts transferred. See **Credit transfer**.

Note that the bank giro credit slip is also used as a *paying-in slip* by a customer paying money into his own account at his own bank branch. Books of these slips are provided by the banks with the customer's name and account number already printed on them.

Bank loan (current account)   Loans can be made to current account holders for a specific reason and for an agreed length of time. Interest is paid on the loan, repayment of which may be by instalments or by a lump sum.

Collateral security may be asked for by the bank for the duration of the loan. It is increasingly common for bank loans to be made to persons who are not customers of a bank.

Bank overdraft (current account)   Permission for current account holders to overdraw on their accounts may be granted by the bank. This permits the drawing on an account of a sum in excess of one's credit at the bank, interest being charged on the day-to-day balance of the overdraft. Collateral security may be asked for by the bank.

Bank paper (stationery)   A cheap variety of paper.

Bank reconciliation statement (banking)   The bank balance shown in the cash book of a firm does not very often agree with the figure shown on a bank statement of the same date. This is quite normal, but it can conceal an error. It is therefore the practice in most firms to arrange to receive daily bank statements which are checked each morning with the balance in the cash book.

A disagreement between the two figures may be due to one of the following—

1   Cheques issued by the firm (and therefore debited in the cash book) may have not been paid in by the payee, or paid in but not yet cleared.

2   The firm may not yet have credited to its account credit transfers, standing orders or direct debits which have already passed through the bank.

3   Bank charges shown by the bank and needing to be entered in the firm's books.

Details of these discrepancies can only be found by checking entries in the cash book individually with items on the bank statement.

When completed the bank reconciliation statement should show in detail the entries causing the discrepancy between the cash book figure and the bank statement.

Bank statements (current and deposit accounts)   See fig 6. The bank statement of account is a copy of the computer account and is given or sent to a customer at regular intervals or when requested. It provides a record of all the transactions of the customer with the bank. Amounts paid out are shown in the payments column, amounts received by the bank for the credit of the account holder are shown in the receipts column. A credit balance therefore is the amount of money that the bank is holding for the account holder, a debit balance shows the amount he owes the

		IN ACCOUNT WITH		
	ARTHUR BROWN, ESQ.,	**BANK OF EDUCATION** HOMETOWN		

DATE	PARTICULARS		PAYMENTS	RECEIPTS	BALANCE
1981	Balance forward				127.43
19 Feb		649	.50		
		648	150.00		23.07DR
24 Feb		CC		300.00	276.93
2 Mar	3% Brit. Treasury	DV		5.00	281.93
5 Mar		BG		50.00	331.93
11 Mar		638	12.00		319.93
12 Mar		650	161.93		158.00
13 Mar	Hometown C.C.	DD	3.25		
	A & B Insce	SO	5.25		149.50
23 Mar		651	25.00		124.50
30 Mar		653	25.00		99.50
31 Mar	Cash Card		10.00		89.50

Account Number	ABBREVIATIONS		Statement Number	
BG Bank Giro Credit	DV Dividend		DR Overdrawn Balance	
DD Direct Debit	CH Charges		SO Standing Order	
CC Cash &/or Chqs	IA Item Advised		TF Inter-Account Transfer	

Fig 6 Bank statement (clearing bank)

bank. Abbreviations are used for most transactions and cheques are identified by their numbers.

Girobank send statements of account, free of charge, to an account holder every time a payment is made into his account, or after there have been 10 payments out since his last statement.

19

Barcharts/bar graphs

Girobank statements of account are sent daily to all businesses.

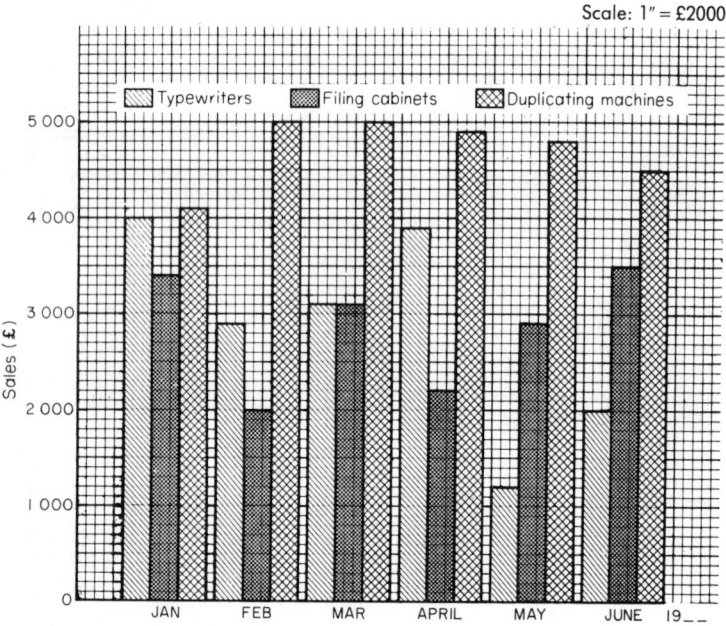

Fig 7 Bar chart/bar graph

Barcharts/bar graphs (communications) See fig 7. These display similar information to that shown by line graphs, but they are more effective for contrasting statistics for defined periods.

Bar coding (computers) Supermarkets commonly use bar code data for pricing and stock updating. The bars on the packet identify the manufacturer and product and are scanned by the cashier at the cash desk. The data is transmitted to a computer that records each item, sends back the price to the sales assistant, reduces the stock level and if necessary creates a requisition or order for further goods to be supplied. Bar codes are increasingly used for recording data on all kinds of stock movement.

Basic pay (salaries and wages). The agreed flat rate paid to an employee for a week, month or year.

Bearer cheques (current account)   These are made out 'Pay Bearer' and are very unsafe. They do not require endorsement and can be cashed by any person presenting them at the counter of the bank branch shown on the cheque.

Bi-chrome ribbon   A typewriter ribbon having two colours, usually black/red.

Bidirectional (word processors)   This describes a printer that prints both when the printing mechanism moves to the right and when it returns.

Bill of exchange (method of payment)   The legal definition of a bill of exchange is that it is 'an unconditional order in writing addressed by one person to another, signed by the person giving it, requiring the person to whom it is addressed to pay on demand, or at a fixed or determinable future time, a certain sum in money to, or to the order of, a specified person or to the bearer'. It is, in effect, a promise to pay a debt to a creditor on a set date (usually in three months' time.) A signed bill of exchange is a legally binding document and banks will accept these bills and pay the holder for them, knowing that on a certain date they can collect the money. The banks' charge for this service is known as a *discount*, and the service itself is known as 'discounting bills of exchange'. The charge is directly related to the current Minimum Lending Rate set by the Bank of England.

Bill of lading This is a paper signed by the master of a ship, by which he makes himself responsible for the safe delivery of the goods specified therein.

Blank cheque (current account) A cheque on which the amount of money to be drawn is not shown. It is advisable to write a monetary limit on such a cheque between the lines of the crossing.

Block (word processors) A group of words, lines or paragraphs which is treated as one unit by the word processor.

Boilerplate (word processors) The American term for standard paragraph.

Bold (word processors) A way of producing text in which each character is darker and thicker than normal.

Bond paper (stationery) A superior quality paper used for business and personal correspondence.

Bonus (salaries and wages) An extra payment made to a person earning money, usually for a specific reason. Some firms give a Christmas bonus to all employees, basing the amount on earnings and/or length of service.

Bookkeeping and accounting machines The basic principles of these machines are the same—simultaneous entry, totalling and balancing. Forms of different sizes and designs can be entered and entries made on them. They draw up accounts neatly and quickly; they are invaluable in firms where the large volume of work to be done would make it impossible to use a manual system.

Box files If it is necessary to keep files in an upright position on shelves, box files should be used, as these are rigid enough to remain in position even if the files on either side are removed. There are three kinds of box file—

1   The papers can be fitted into the box by means of a loose-leaf book and kept secure by means of a lever-arch clip.

2   Loose papers are held in the box by a strong clip. This is used mainly for papers awaiting attention which will be filed later in a permanent place. The vouchers for petty cash payments are often kept in this way until they have been entered up.

3   The third type is simply a box with a lift-up lid. When the lid is raised one side of the box can be dropped to allow easier access to the papers.

Bring forward system   See **Follow-up systems**.

British telecom (communications)   This used to be a part of the Post Office but is now an independent organisation which provides all public telecommunication services such as telephones, Telex, etc.

British telecom international (BTI)   The international division of British Telecom.

Budget account (banking and girobank)   A budget account will enable a bank customer to spread his payments more evenly. For instance, all household expenses (mortgage payments, gas, electricity, telephone, holidays, etc) may be totalled for the year, and the total divided by 12. Each month this figure is taken out of the current account of the householder and placed in a budget account which has a *separate cheque-book*. The householder can draw on this account up to three times the monthly figure. In this way the months when quarterly bills come in can be cleared immediately, and during months when there are no large bills the account balances itself out. An annual charge is made for this service.

Buffer (word processors)   The name given to the part of the word processor's memory that holds text.

Bundled (word processors)   Describes a system in which everything is included in one price.

Bureau (word processors)   A company that provides the services of a word processor, and expertise.

Business card/visiting card   A visitor from another firm may offer the receptionist a business/visiting card showing his or her name, firm, and position in the firm.

Business diary (appointments)   It is essential that an entry is made in the diary of every appointment or interview arranged, and in the diary (or some other follow-up system) of every matter requiring attention at a later date.

The most usual form of diary for executivies and their secretaries is the 'page-a-day' desk diary, which may be obtained with half- or quarter-hour times already printed. The bottom part of the page is often left blank for notes, and can be used for reminders.

It is usual for both executive and secretary to keep their own diaries, and it is essential that the secretary makes sure that all entries appear in both. This requires daily checking to avoid the possibility of double bookings; times of meetings should be entered as soon as they are known, even if the date is a long way ahead.

Business directory   A reference book with lists of inhabitants of districts, members of professions, etc, with various details.

Foreign telephone directories are available from British Telecom.

The *Girobank Business Accounts Directory* lists Girobank Business Account numbers.

Local classified directories of businesses and services are printed independently and distributed free of charge to all premises in the area (eg *Thomson's*)

Postcode directories are available free of charge to businesses and large users of the post.

All *telephone directories* are available from British Telecom. *Local* directories are provided free for each subscriber.

A *telephone dialling code directory* is issued to every subscriber.

A *Telex directory* is issued to all Telex subscribers listing all Telex numbers.

The *Yellow Pages* is a form of business directory; it lists telephone subscribers in the relevant area according to trade or profession.

Business documents (transactions) The following is a comprehensive list of documents used in a business transaction; obviously no transaction would entail using every one. Usually the top copy is sent to the addressee and a varying number of copies are kept by the issuing firm for different purposes—accounts and stock records, for instance. The order of the list below is that of the order in which the forms would be used. Information on each will be found under separate headings in this dictionary, and a complete description of a transaction under **Transactions**.

1 Enquiry
2 Estimate
3 Quotation
4 Tender
5 Firm offer
6 Order
7 Despatch note
8 Advice note
9 Delivery note
10 Packing note
11 Consignment note
12 Invoice
13 Pro forma invoice
14 Credit note
15 Debit note
16 Statement of account
17 Remittance advice
18 Receipt

Business letters (communications) See fig 8. *Headed paper* is used for business letters. The following items usually appear:

Business letters

Date—Today's, 'date for tomorrow', date as postmark
Your reference—The addressee's reference ⎱(Usually file
Our reference—The writer's reference ⎰references)
Confidential or *Personal* if required
Addressee's name and address
For the attention of——if required
Salutation—Dear Sir, Dear Madam, Dear Occupier
Subject heading—indicates what the letter has been written about
Body of the letter—Usually made up of three parts—
1   Reason for writing the letter
2   Action to be taken or about to be taken. (This may involve several paragraphs.)
3   Future action to be taken, or if letter closes the correspondence a suitable final sentence, 'Thank you for your assistance in this matter', or similar sentence.
Complimentary close (*subscription*)—
Yours faithfully or Yours truly (if the letter starts with Dear Sir or Dear Madam).
    or
Yours sincerely (if the letter starts Dear Mr Smith or Dear John).
(occasionally) *Name of firm or organisation*—typed immediately under 'Yours . . .'
Space for signature above the writer's name which is *typed* immediately above the
Designation—the position in the firm or organisation of the writer of the letter.
(occasionally) *per procurationem*, abbreviated pp or per pro. In business authority is sometimes given to certain officials to sign on behalf of another employee. When signing 'per pro' the signature should appear *below* the name of the person taking responsibility for the letter.
Enc(s)—if any matter is to be enclosed with the letter.
NB *Continuation sheets*—If business letters extend beyond

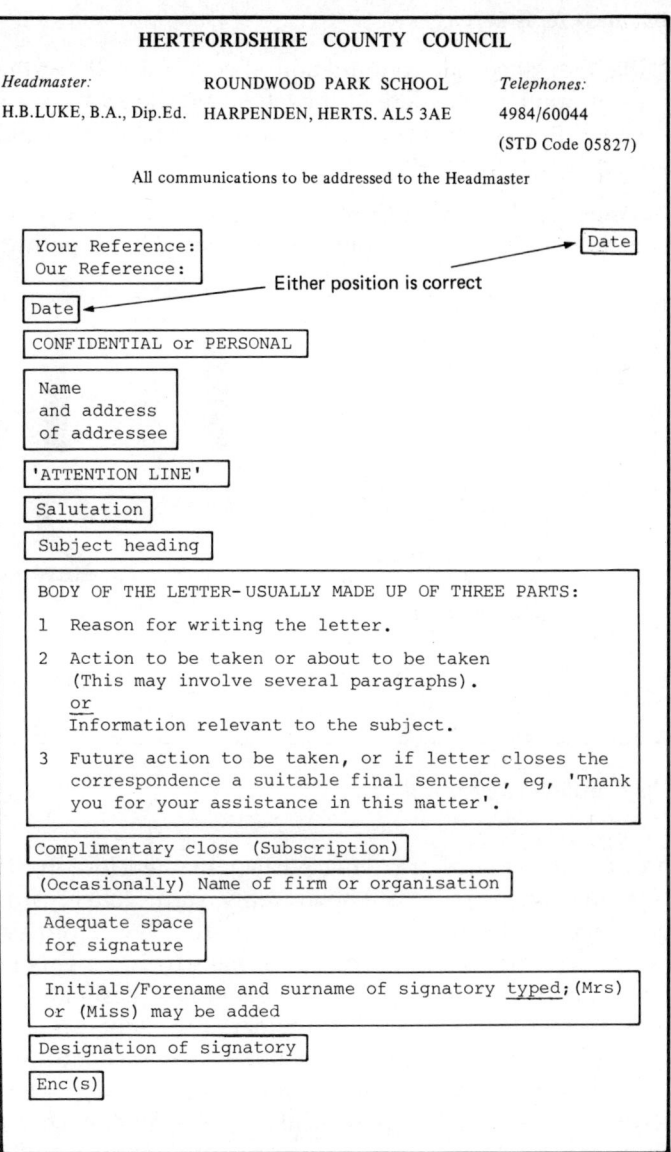

HERTFORDSHIRE COUNTY COUNCIL

Headmaster: ROUNDWOOD PARK SCHOOL *Telephones:*
H.B.LUKE, B.A., Dip.Ed. HARPENDEN, HERTS. AL5 3AE 4984/60044
(STD Code 05827)

All communications to be addressed to the Headmaster

Your Reference:
Our Reference:
→ Date

Either position is correct

Date ←

CONFIDENTIAL or PERSONAL

Name
and address
of addressee

'ATTENTION LINE'

Salutation

Subject heading

BODY OF THE LETTER- USUALLY MADE UP OF THREE PARTS:

1 Reason for writing the letter.

2 Action to be taken or about to be taken
   (This may involve several paragraphs).
   or
   Information relevant to the subject.

3 Future action to be taken, or if letter closes the
   correspondence a suitable final sentence, eg, 'Thank
   you for your assistance in this matter'.

Complimentary close (Subscription)

(Occasionally) Name of firm or organisation

Adequate space
for signature

Initials/Forename and surname of signatory typed; (Mrs)
or (Miss) may be added

Designation of signatory

Enc(s)

Fig 8 Layout of a business letter

27

Business reply service

the first sheet all continuation sheets must show the page number, the date of the letter and the addressee's name. It is not necessary to show his address on second or subsequent sheets of a letter.

Business reply service (Royal Mail)   See fig 9. A person who wishes to obtain a reply from a client without putting

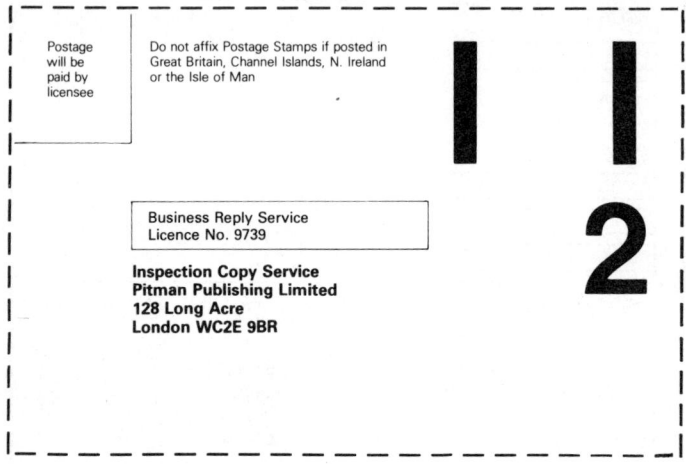

Postage will be paid by licensee

Do not affix Postage Stamps if posted in Great Britain, Channel Islands, N. Ireland or the Isle of Man

Business Reply Service
Licence No. 9739

Inspection Copy Service
Pitman Publishing Limited
128 Long Acre
London WC2E 9BR

Fig 9 Business reply card

him to the expense of paying postage may enclose in his communication an unstamped reply card, letter card, envelope, folder or gummed label bearing the approved design. He may also incorporate in his advertisements in newspapers and other publications a special design to be used as an address label or as a folder. The client can post the card, etc, in the ordinary way but without a stamp; and the addressee will pay the charges on all the replies received. The replies may be sent as either first or second class mail. The service may be used by anyone who obtains a licence, though it is chiefly designed for business firms and advertisers. An annual licence fee is payable.

Business units   An organisation doing business is a business unit. The type of unit it is can be determined by asking two questions: who provided the *capital* (and therefore 'owns' it) and who receives the *profits*.

In the United Kingdom we have a 'mixed economy' which means that some organisations are privately owned, while some are publicly owned and run by the Government or Local Authorities.

The following is a list of the different types of business unit:

PRIVATE SECTOR
Sole trader—owns and runs his or her own business and takes all the profits.
Partnership—usually owned and run by two or more partners, who receive the profits.
Private limited company—owned by the shareholders, who receive the profits, and whose shares are *not* sold publicly.
Public limited company—owned by the shareholders, who receive the profits, and whose shares are sold on the stock exchange.
Holding company—a more sophisticated type of public limited company.

NON-PROFITMAKING UNITS (in the private sector)
Co-operative societies—retail and wholesale.
Friendly societies—eg building societies.
Many different clubs and societies.

PUBLIC SECTOR
Central government departments (eg the Department of Health and Social Security, the Department of Education and Science)—headed by Ministers who are Members of

29

Parliament, and funded through the collection of taxes and national insurance.

Public corporations which administer public services such as British Rail, British Steel, etc. They are each controlled by a Board which is responsible to a Government Minister.

Local Government

County councils: There are 39 non-Metropolitan County Councils, 6 Metropolitan County Councils, plus the Greater London Council. The Metropolitan County Councils control heavily populated areas, exemplified by the West Midlands and Greater Manchester. County Councils provide services such as education, social services and libraries and are funded partly from rates and partly from Government funds.

All the County Councils are arranged into districts, served by *District Councils*. The most important function of District Councils is the provision of housing, various environmental or public health functions, maintenance of sewers, refuse collection, street-cleansing, etc. (Note that the Greater London Council is divided into *boroughs*). To provide these local services the District Councils rely entirely on the money collected from ratepayers. For many other services the local authority makes a charge in order to cover costs; among these are swimming pools, threatres, leisure centres, etc.

Byte (computers)   One character.

C

In the Telephone Alphabet C is for Charlie

Abbreviations

CA	Chartered Accountant
c & f.	cost and freight
caps.	capitals
CB	cash book
cd.	could
c/d	carried down
cf	compare (from Latin *confer*)
cfi.	cost, freight and insurance
cm	centimetre
co.	company
c/o	care of
COD	cash on delivery
COM	computer output on microfilm
CPI	characters per inch
CPS.	characters per second
CPU	central processing unit
cr	credit, creditor
CRT.	cathode ray tube
C/T	credit transfer
CV	curriculum vitae
CWO	cash with order

Calculating machines These have been developed to carry out the processes of multiplication and division besides addition and subtraction.

Calculators   Electronic calculators with printing facilities are commonly used in offices for tasks which involve calculations. The tally roll provides printed proof, and can be kept for future reference. Equally common are the small portable electronic calculators with LED screen and memory which can be used for a variety of arithmetical processes.

Callmaker (British Telecom)   British Telecom offer several different types of callmaker, all of which store frequently used telephone numbers, and enable the subscriber to save time when making telephone calls.
Card callmakers use cards which are hole-punched with a telephone number, each card being capable of recording up to 16 digits; one is prepared for each telephone number. By slipping the correct card into the slot of a callmaker unit the number will be dialled automatically.
The *tape callmaker* can store up to 400 numbers on magnetic tape, each with up to 18 digits. To make a call the power-driven tape is moved along until the number required appears on the indicator; by pressing the 'call' button the call is connected.

Carbon (duplicating)   Until recently the most common method of copying a document at the time of preparation was by means of carbon paper; the term *manifolding* was applied to the making of several copies of the same matter in this way. With ordinary standard weight carbon paper about four clear copies could be made with a typewriter, and two copies with a hard pencil or ballpoint pen, copies of business letters being made on flimsy paper.
Photocopiers are rapidly making the use of carbon paper for copies of business letters obsolete.
Hectograph carbon (also known as a transfer sheet) is used in the preparation of spirit masters.

Carboned stationery   Forms with carboned stationery which retains the carbon coating are used with continuous stationery machines.

Carbon ribbon (typewriters)   Carbon ribbons give a high-quality finish to typewritten work, but have the disadvantage that they can only be used once. They are attached to the typewriter by an additional ribbon carrier into which the ribbon spool is easily slotted.

Card index   A method of arranging cards containing names and addresses or other information in a classified order.

Card index reminder   See **Follow-up systems**.

Cardphone (British Telecom)   The cardphone employs the latest microprocessor technology to provide a speedy, convenient and efficient way of making calls without using cash. The user inserts a slim phonecard and dials the number required. Once connected, units will be automatically removed from the phonecard as the call proceeds. Phonecards can be obtained from any post office showing the phonecard sign.

Carriage forward   This means that the cost of carriage is paid by the buyer.

Carriage paid   This means that the cost of carriage is paid by the seller.

Carriage return (word processors)   A key used to mark the end of a line or paragraph of text. Often just called **Return**.

Carried unanimously (meetings)   A motion is said to be 'carried unanimously' when all members present at the meeting have voted in favour of it. (See also **Nem con**).

Cartridge disk (word processors)   A large, high-capacity disk housed in a round plastic cartridge.

Cartridge ribbon (word processors/computers)   A printer ribbon which is contained in a plastic cartridge. This makes it easy to remove and replace.

Cash   Coins and notes of the realm.

Cash analysis (salaries and wages)   The numbers of different denominations of notes and coins required from the bank for payroll payments.

Cash book (accounts)   The Cash and Bank Accounts of a firm are kept side-by-side in a double column cash-book. It is the responsibility of the cashier to ensure that every amount of money received or paid out by the firm is recorded in this book.

Cash card (current account)   See fig 10. This enables bank customers to obtain money from cash dispensers outside banking hours.
Holders of a Midland Bank eurocheque card may withdraw local currency from over 500 cash dispensers throughout Spain.

Cash discount (transactions)   This is given to debtors who pay promptly for goods when the time for payment arrives—eg, '2½% discount for payment within one month'. Also known as **settlement discount**.

Cash dispenser (current account)   This is a machine set in the wall of a bank branch or retail store as well as inside bank premises, which is stocked with bank notes. The bank customer is given a secret personal code number and a card which when inserted into the machine activates a keyboard; the customer may then tap out his number and the amount of cash required. Each customer is set either a weekly or daily limit for withdrawals using a dispenser. Besides providing cash some machines give customers the balance remaining in their current account, and will also accept requests for bank statements (current account only), which will be forwarded to the customer.

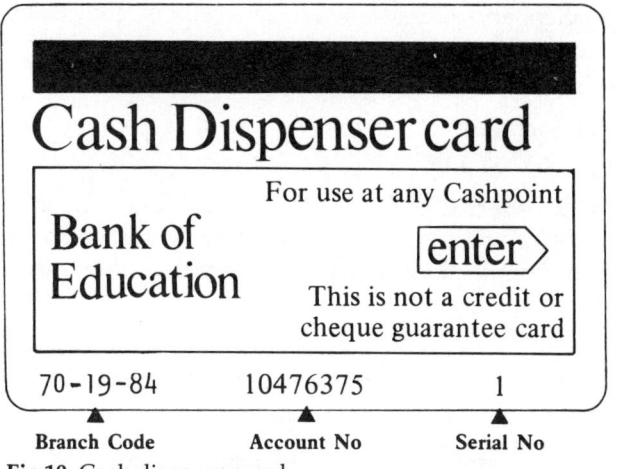

Fig 10 Cash dispenser card

Cash dispenser card (current account)   See fig 10. This enables bank customers to obtain money from Cash Dispensers outside banking hours.

Holders of a Midland Bank eurocheque card may withdraw local currency from over 500 cash dispensers throughout Spain. (See fig 19.)

Cash on delivery (COD)   (Royal Mail method of payment) Under this service the amount called the COD amount or trade charge—specified by the sender for collection on delivery of a parcel, first class letter or packet—can, on certain conditions, be collected from the addressee by the postman and remitted to the sender. All letters and packets must be registered. The COD amount will normally be sent to the creditor by means of a Girobank cheque. Exporters can send parcels by the COD Overseas Service to 58 countries from main post offices.

Cash register (office machinery)   The sales department of a business requires information regarding the amount of money taken, and at the same time a receipt is required by the customer. A cash register will perform both functions, and will produce an analysis of the figures if required.

Cash transaction   This involves immediate payment for goods or services purchased.

Cash with order (CWO) (method of payment)   Usually requested in advertisements, and is a safe method from the advertiser's point of view. Cheques or postal orders may be sent with such orders.

Casting vote (meetings)   When the 'for' and 'against' votes taken at a meeting are equal, the Chairman has a 'casting vote' which will decide the issue.

Catalogue (transactions)   A catalogue is generally intended for use over a considerable time and is therefore a more elaborate production than a price list. Mail order customers can order by post or telephone from such catalogues.

Centralised filing department   A central filing department can offer the following advantages:
1   It stores all files in one location which is known to all employees.
2   It employes a specialist filing staff.
3   It can afford to invest in specialist equipment and labour-saving devices.
4   It enjoys the benefits of uniformity of method.
5   It provides greater management control.
The system is an alternative to departmental filing (qv).

Central processing unit/CPU (computers)   Now made of microchips, this part of the computer contains the memory. The data in the memory is also processed in the CPU.

Centring (word processors)   Putting a line of text, such as a heading, in the middle of the screen or paper, between the margin settings.

Certificate of pay, tax deducted and National Insurance contributions (P60)   This is the third copy of the P14 which is made out annually by employers for each employee. It is a proof that income tax and National Insurance contributions have been paid for the year shown. This is an important document and should be carefully kept; *duplicates cannot be obtained*. (See fig 34.)

Certificate of posting (Royal Mail)   A certificate of posting may be obtained at any post office counter for any unregistered letter, packet or parcel, when proof is required that the item has been posted to a particular person.

Change/exchange form (current account)   This form is used in the following three ways:
1   For exchanging small change for larger denominations or notes.
2   For exchanging bank notes/coins of large denomination for small change.
3   When accompanied by a cheque for cash it stipulates the particulars of cash required. This is necessary when the salaries or wages of a number of different persons are to be paid in cash; it ensures that sufficient amounts of the right notes and small change are available to pay each employee with the exact amount of money required.

Character (computers)   A letter, number, space, mark or symbol.

Character formation (word processors) The way a character is displayed on a screen or printed on paper. On the screen, a character is made up of tiny dots of light. On paper it is fully formed—ie, not made up of dots.

Character set (word processors) The total range of characters that can be displayed on a screen or printed on paper.

Charts Bar charts, flowcharts and pie charts, line graphs and pictograms are all used in offices to display essential facts and figures in a way which can be quickly assimilated.

Cheque (current account) See figs 11 and 12. A cheque is a method of payment through the clearing banks.

Essentials of a cheque
Cheques can be accepted for clearing (ie, the money transferred from the payer's (drawer's) account either to the payee or into his account) only if the following five items appear:
1 *the date*—A cheque must be dated. (See 'stale' and 'post-dated' cheques under Types of cheque, below).
2 *the payee's name* (unless it is made out to Cash by the owner of the account who intends to cash it at his own bank branch).
3/4 *the amount* which must be written in *words* and in *figures* with no discrepancy between the two.
5 *the drawer's signature.*

Parties to a cheque
There are always three parties to a cheque:
1 *The drawer* (payer), who is the one who signs the cheque.
2 *The drawee*, who is always the banker.
3 The *payee*, who receives payment.

Crossed cheque   Bank and branch code number

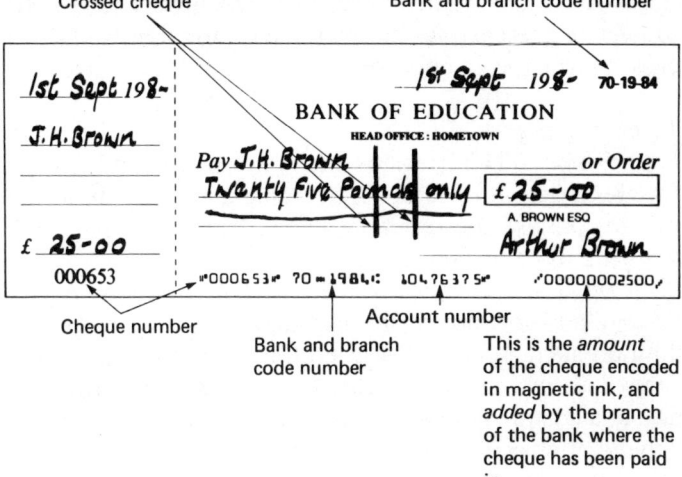

Cheque number

Bank and branch code number

Account number

This is the *amount* of the cheque encoded in magnetic ink, and *added* by the branch of the bank where the cheque has been paid in.

Fig 11 Crossed cheque

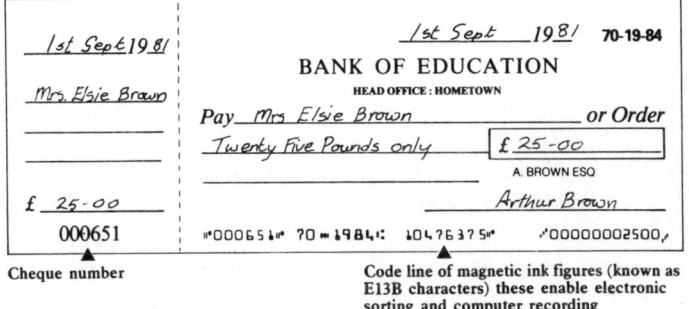

Cheque number

Code line of magnetic ink figures (known as E13B characters) these enable electronic sorting and computer recording

Fig 12 Open cheque

Returned cheques

Cheques returned to the payee by the bank may be marked

1 R/D—Refer to Drawer
2 I/F—Insufficient Funds
3 N/F—No Funds

Cheques

In all cases the cheques should be referred back to the drawer of the cheque—he may have forgotten to date or sign the cheque in question.

Types of cheque
Bearer cheque—This is made out 'Pay Bearer' and is very unsafe. It does not require endorsement and can be cashed by any person presenting it at the counter of the bank branch shown on the cheque.

Blank cheque—A cheque on which the amount of money to be drawn is not shown. It is advisable to write a monetary limit on such a cheque between the lines of the crossing.

Crossed cheque—If two parallel lines are drawn across the face of a cheque it must be paid into a bank account; this is a 'general crossing'. (See fig 11.)

A/c payee only (Account payee only) appearing between the lines means that it can be paid only into the account of the payee. Occasionally the bank and branch of the payee's account are also clearly stated—this is known as a 'special crossing'.

Eurocheque—Midland Bank is presently the only major UK clearing Bank to issue eurocheques to their customers for use when travelling for business or on holiday. They can be used in 39 European and Mediterranean countries and can be written in most European currencies.

Open cheque—This has no crossing and can be paid over the bank counter of the bank branch printed on it. (See fig 12.)

Post-dated cheque—A cheque made payable on a later date than the present date. It will not be cleared until the date shown.

Stale cheque—A cheque is stale if it is more than six months old in which case it may not be accepted by the bank.

Traveller's cheque—The traveller's cheque provides a safe and convenient way of carrying money, and is ideally suited to the holiday-maker and traveller. Traveller's cheques may be cashed not only at the branches of all the main banks in the British Isles, but also in most banks abroad, and they are frequently accepted at hotels and by large shops.

Anyone can buy traveller's cheques and they are available in denominations of £5, £10, £20, £50, £100. At the time of purchasing, each cheque must be signed at the foot ('signature of drawer'). When presented for payment, it must be signed again, ('drawer's endorsement') and dated in the presence of the paying agent.

It is also possible to purchase traveller's cheques drawn in a foreign currency.

Mistakes made in the writing of a cheque
If a mistake is made in the writing of a cheque the drawer should sign his name as near as possible to the alteration, in addition to his usual signature.

To stop payment of a cheque (See fig 13)
The drawer of a cheque may wish to stop payment if he learns that the cheque has been lost, or if, for some reason, he does not wish the particular payment to be made. To stop a cheque a form is filled in and presented to the bank branch of issue. Bank staff are requested to keep a careful watch for the cheque, but, as a safeguard, a record of the 'Stop' is placed on the computer file of the account holder. A stop cannot be placed on a cheque issued under a cheque card.

Endorsing (*over*) is the signing of one's name on the back of a cheque. This must be done when a cheque is paid into the account of a person who is not the named payee of the cheque.

Cheque card (current account)   See fig 14. A cheque card is a guarantee by the issuing bank branch that it will pay cheques drawn in association with the card up to a

---

TO   **BANK OF EDUCATION**

   HOMETOWN   BRANCH   DATE *1st Sept 1981*

PLEASE **STOP** payment of the undermentioned cheque:

   ACCOUNT   *A·Brown   No.10476375*

   CHEQUE NO. *000659*   DATED *1st Aug 1981*

   PAYEE   *A·B·C· Co·Ltd·*

   AMOUNT £ *56-62*

   CROSSED/~~OPEN~~   *Not Negotiable*

until further instructions are received from me in writing. I certify that this
cheque was not issued in conjunction with my cheque card.

                    Arthur Brown   Customer's Signature

(BANK USE ONLY)

                        DATE AND TIME OF RECEIPT

            RECORDED

                        RECORDS VERIFIED

                                    Manager's Assistant

Fig 13 Stopping payment of a cheque

specified limit for any one transaction. As a means of
identification it shows the name and specimen signature of
the holder, the card serial number and the date of expiry.
The card may be used:

a To enable the holder to encash a cheque up to a
specified limit at any branch of any bank within the
scheme.

b To support a cheque up to a specified value. Any
payees accepting a cheque under the terms of a cheque
card, can rely on the cheque being paid, provided the rules
governing the use of the card are observed. It is not

possible to 'stop' payment of any cheque issued under a cheque card.

Current account customers who wish to issue cheques abroad must obtain an additional *eurocheque card*; the cheque card issued for use in the United Kingdom is not valid overseas.

Fig 14 Cheque card

The eurocheque card issued by the Midland Bank can be used to withdraw local currency from over 500 *cash dispensers* throughout Spain; it is hoped that in the near future the service will be expanded to cover some 19 different countries.

Cheque-writing machine　This machine operates in much the same way as an ordinary typewriter, but instead of merely printing on the surface of the paper the typeface cuts impressions into the paper, thus making alterations to the typed matter impossible.

Chronological filing　One of the five main filing systems: papers are filed in date order, the most recent papers usually being on the top.

Chronological order   Filing in the order of the date which appears on the letter or document.

Circular letters   These are duplicated letters sent to several addresses.
1   Either addressed generally—Dear Sir, Dear Madam, Dear Householder, etc.
   or
2   Addressed individually. In this case a space is left for the addressee's name and address, and in the salutation (Dear . . .).
If a very large number of circulars is to be posted use can be made of the Printed Postage Impression facility offered by the Royal Mail (qv).

Circulation slip   This is also known as a **Routing slip**.
When there is only one copy of a document which must be read by several people a circulation list of the names of the people concerned is attached to it, and it is then sent to the person whose name appears at the top of the list. When he has read or acted upon it he will sign against his name and pass the document on to the next person named.
When all signatures have been collected the document is returned to the originator.
Circulation lists may be prepared for individual documents, or each department may keep its own comprehensive list from which names may be deleted as appropriate before circulation of a particular document.

Classified trades directory   Local classified directories of businesses and services, with street maps, are published independently and distributed to all premises in an area. (eg Thomson's *Local Directories*).
The *Yellow Pages* distributed by British Telecom to all telephone subscribers form a classified business directory which is complementary to the local telephone directory. It

lists telephone subscribers in the local area according to trade or profession.

Clearing banks' methods of payment The following methods of payment use the services offered by the clearing banks: banker's credit card, banker's draft, bank giro credit system, cheque, credit transfer, direct debit, standing order. See also **Banking**.

Clerical function and the duties of office staff The clerical function involves writing, copying, computing, checking, filing and indexing, sorting, and all forms of communication.
Employees engaged in the clerical function are known as *clerks*.

Clerk Any employee who performs the clerical function of writing, copying, computing, checking, filing and indexing, and sorting, is a clerk.
The word is usually preceded by an adjective describing the nature of the position held—eg Junior Clerk, Senior Clerk, Stores Clerk, Accounts Clerk, Clerk/Typist etc.

Clockcard (salaries and wages) If the 'clocking on' system is used each worker is given a Time- or Clockcard which he inserts into the time-recording machine on arrival at and departure from his place of work. This records automatically the correct time, which appears on the card. The cards are kept in racks by the side of the clock, and are used in assessing overtime, punctuality, etc. If the cards are numbered the number is referred to as the 'clock number', and is often used as the reference number of that particular worker by the personnel department.

Code (word processors) A system in which letters, numbers or other symbols are arbitrarily assigned a meaning.

Code number (income tax)   Number given by the Inspector of Taxes to every wage or salary earner to enable his employer to work out how much income tax he must deduct.

Coding claim (P15)   This income tax form will be given to an employee who has no code number, possibly because he cannot get a P45 or has lost it, or because he is earning money for the first time. (See fig 32.)

Coin analysis/coin and note summaries (salaries and wages)   The float in a shop till at the beginning of the day, or in the Petty Cash account, should consist of a mixture of notes and coins of different denominations. The shopkeeper or Petty Cashier will learn from experience how the money should be ordered, and will show the different amounts required on the change/exchange form accompanying the cheque.

When the salaries or wages of a number of different persons are to be paid in cash, sufficient amounts of the right notes and coins should be available to pay each employee with the exact amount of money required. This must be worked out in advance and the analysis shown on the change/exchange form accompanying the cheque.

Collateral security   A person borrowing from a bank by means of a loan or overdraft may be asked to offer some sort of security. This might take the form, for instance, of the deeds of a house, and is known as collateral—ie security lying alongside the debt. See **Bank loan** and **Bank overdraft**.

Collating machines   When a report running into many pages has been duplicated the sets have to be sorted and stapled together (collated). These machines can complete the task very quickly, particularly when linked to a photocopying machine. When this is done duplicating and collating are achieved in one operation.

Committee (meetings) Several people selected from a more numerous body (such as a club, association or society) to which the special business of running the organisation is committed. The committee and officers of the committee are elected at the Annual General Meeting of the organisation. Members of a Committee attend regular meetings at which the activities of the organisation are discussed and decisions taken. The *elected officers* of such committees are normally the Chairman, Treasurer and Secretary.

Communications This word covers all the ways used to transmit information, ideas, or feelings from one person to another or others.

Communications (word processors) An additional unit of hardware, which when coupled with some software, enables a word processor to exchange text or other information with other equipment, such as Telexes, or other word processors.

Company secretary Every limited company, however small, must have a Secretary, whose job it is to ensure that the business complies with the provisions of the Companies Acts. The Company Secretary's Department is also responsible for the keeping of registers, books and records, the preparation of documents, and the issue of shares. He or she must also keep shareholders informed of the financial position of the firm and notify them of meetings, for which he or she must afterwards produce and circulate the minutes. In many firms the Company Secretary's Department is responsible for the provision of office services.

Compensation fee parcel service (Royal Mail) See fig 15. Payment of a fee when posting a parcel at the Post Office

The Post Office

Certificate of Posting for Compensation Fee Parcel

How to post

1. Enter below in ink the name and full address as written on the parcel.
2. Tick the appropriate box at the bottom of the form to indicate the compensation cover required.

Name

Address

Postcode

Stamps for Compensation Fee
(to be cancelled by accepting officer)

For Post Office use

COD Deposit/
Inpayment Document No

Compensation Fee Paid

p

Accepting Officer's initials

Date stamp

Tick compensation cover required

Up to £60 ☐

Up to £125 ☐

Up to £225 ☐

Up to £350 ☐

PP89 Feb 84

Fig 15 Compensation fee certificate of posting (parcels)

counter covers the contents of any inland parcel for compensation in the event of damage or loss, and provides a record of postage. The cost is relative to the value of the parcel.

Pitman Publishing Ltd

128 Long Acre, London WC2E 9AN

Telephone: 01-379 7383

With Compliments

Fig 16 Compliment slip

Compliment slip   See fig 16. When material is sent out which does not need a covering letter it is usual to accompany such material with a compliment slip. This shows the name and address of the firm sending the material, and sometimes short messages are written or typed on it.

Complimentary close (business letters)   The phrase beginning 'Yours . . .' at the end of a letter. Also known as the *subscription*.

Compound interest   Interest added to the principal at the end of each period (usually a year), forming a new principal for the next period on which interest is calculated. See also **Simple interest**.

Computers   General-purpose electronic machines for processing information. A computer forms the basis of a word
processor.

Computers need instructions from trained personnel. The
instructions are called *programs*, and are written by *computer programmers* using *programming languages* (eg Basic,
Cobol etc).

These programs are the *software* of the computer system,
and the computer equipment is called the *hardware*.

The use of computers in the automated office is increasing
daily. Among the many uses are: airline and hotel reservations, customer records in banks and building societies
(including cash dispenser usage), databases, management
information systems, payroll systems, and stock records
and control.

Viewdata is a system whereby information stored in a
computer (or in many computers) can be called up by
telephone and displayed on the screen. See **Prestel**.

Computer hardware   This is the computer equipment and
has four main parts:

1 *Input devices*   The most common method used in
offices to input data is by way of a keyboard connected to a
terminal and linked to the computer. Other methods
include: OMR (optical marks as on multiple choice examination answers); OCR (optical character recognition
were specially shaped characters can be recognised by the
computer equipment); MICR (magnetic ink character recognition as used on cheques); bar codes as at supermarket
point of sales.

2 *Central processing unit*   Now made of microchips, this
part of the computer contains the memory. The data in the
memory is also processed in the central processing unit
(CPU).

3 *Output devices*   Processed data can be output from the

computer in a number of forms: eg on paper using a *printer*; on the screen of a *VDU* (visual display unit); on microfilm—*COM* (computer output on microfilm).

4 *Backing store* Data or programs currently in the memory can be kept. Examples of backing store are floppy disks, rigid disks, magnetic tapes and cassette tapes.

Computer software This is the programs, ie the sets of instructions used by the computer.

Concertina file This is a portable folder which when opened presents a series of compartments. Also known as an **expanding file**.

Conference call (British Telecom) This service enables three or more people to take part in one telephone conversation. It is useful for business discussions.

Confidential mail (business letters) If a letter is of a confidential nature the word CONFIDENTIAL should appear above the address on both letters and envelopes. Letters so marked, when received by a firm's Mailing Department, should be passed to the addressee unopened.

Configuration (word processors) General term given to the arrangement of physical units within a system.

Confravision (British Telecom) An inter-city conference service available from studios in London, Birmingham, Bristol, Glasgow, Manchester, Leeds and Ipswich. It provides black and white vision plus sound communication between two groups in their respective cities. Among the advantages are the avoidance of: travel time and of possible late arrival, travel fatigue, and prolonged absence from base of heavily committed executives.

Consequential loss insurance with the inland registered post (Royal Mail) Consequential loss is a loss to the user of the post arising out of some failure in the postal service—a loss over and above the actual value of the article lost, damaged or delayed. For instance, the loss of a passport in the post could mean a delayed business trip and the loss of an important contract. Consequential Loss Insurance incurs a cost additional to the registration fee and first class postage, and is dependent on the amount of compensation cover required.

Consignment   All the goods delivered at any one time, whether all or part of an order.

Consignment note (transactions)   Note sent covering all the goods delivered at any one time.

Consumable stock (stock records)   Stock which will be used up and need regular replacement, such as stationery items (notebooks, pencils, paper clips etc).

Continuation sheets (business letters)   If business letters extend beyond the first sheet all continuation sheets must show the page number, the date of the letter and the addressee's name. It is not necessary to show the address on second or subsequent sheets of a letter.

Continuous stationery machine   With a machine of this type it is possible to feed invoices or forms into a type-writer from the rear and tear them off as completed. As each set of forms is finished the next automatically follows on. At the flick of a lever the carbon from the completed set is automatically fed into the next set at the correct position for typing, unless the forms are carboned stationery which retains the carbon coating.

Contract of employment (Personnel Department)   Under the Contracts of Employment Act 1972 every employer is obliged to give every employee a written statement of the main terms of his or her employment within thirteen weeks of starting work. This must show:

1   Names of employer and employee.
2   Date of commencement of employment.
3   Rate of pay.
4   Whether weekly or monthly paid.
5   Hours of work.
6   Conditions relating to pay when absent through sickness.
7   Pension rights.
8   Length of notice to be given by either side to terminate the contract.
9   Holidays and payment for holidays.
10   The right to belong to a trade union.
11   The right not to belong to a trade union.
12   The procedures for registering a grievance.
13   The steps of the subsequent grievance procedure.

Co-operative   Productive co-operatives are societies of workers who provide the capital to organise their own factories. They sometimes arise when factories are faced with closure, and the workers pool their resources to keep the factory going. Profits are divided equally.

Agricultural co-operatives are formed by groups of farmers or growers who between them finance the purchase of processing-plant and distribution centres; profits are shared by the owners.

Co-operative societies   The co-operative retail societies (CRS) own many shops and supermarkets; the CWS (Co-operative Wholesale Society) supplies the CRS shops. All the co-operative retail shops are owned by the members who contribute £1 shares (up to a maximum of £5000) on which interest is paid. Dividend is paid to customers on goods purchased by the issue of Co-operative Trading Stamps.

The Co-operative Wholesale Society is owned by the co-operative retail shops.

Copy (block) (word processors)   A procedure to move a block of text from one location to another within the text. The block is not deleted from its original position.

Copying (reprographics)   Photocopiers can produce a replica of an original document, but if duplicating machines are used (eg spirit, ink/stencil, or offset-litho), a master must be prepared from which copies can be made.

Copy-typist   A copy-typist does not use shorthand or audio equipment, and types from manuscripts or 'copy'. The good copy-typist is a touch typist who is fast and accurate and able to produce effective display work. Copy-typists are often employed in typing pools where the supply of work is regulated by a supervisor.

Correcting fluid (duplicating)   This is manufactured for use with spirit masters or stencils. If an error is made, the wrong characters are coated over with the fluid, which when dry can be typed over. In the case of stencils for ink duplicating the fluid is painted on the typing surface; with spirit masters the back of the master must be treated.

Correction signs   Fig 17 is a table of the most common correction signs used in manuscripts.

Correspondence (communications)   This can mean:
1   All communication by letter and documentation.
2   The complete set of letters on one particular subject, usually collected together in one file (a correspondence file).

Corruption (word processors)   The inadvertent destruction of text on a disk, by exposure to stray magnetic fields.

Counterfoil   The part of a postal order, cheque, ticket, etc, which is retained by the giver to provide a record. Also called a *stub*.

No	Correction	Sign in margin	Sign in text
1	Insert full stop	⊙	λ
2	Insert colon	(:)	λ
3	Insert comma	,/	λ
4	Insert semi-colon	;/	λ
5	Insert question mark	?/	λ
6	Insert exclamation mark	!/	λ
7	Insert apostrophe	’7	λ
8	Insert quotation marks	“7 ”7	λ λ
9	Insert hyphen	|-|	λ
10	Insert dash	/–/	λ
11	Insert brackets	(/)/	λ λ
12	Insert square brackets	[/]/	λ λ
13	Use capital letters	Caps	≡
14	Use small capital letters	SC	=
15	Underline word(s)	Underline	—
16	Insert word(s)	Words to be inserted /	λ
17	Use italics	ital	—
18	Use Roman type	Rom	encircle word(s)
19	Use bold type	Bold	~~~
20	Use lower case letters	lc	encircle letter(s)
21	Transpose words or letters	trs	⊔⊓
22	Delete	∂	Word(s) or Letter(s) crossed out
23	To remain as it was before correction	Stet	---------- under word(s) to remain
24	Space required	#	λ
25	Equalise the spacing	eq #	λ
26	Close up the space	⁐	⁐
27	Start a new paragraph	NP	[
28	Continue without a new paragraph	Run on	⟶
29	Improve damaged character	×	encircle character
30	Wrong fount	w.f.	encircle character
31	Letter upside down	9	encircle character
32	Move to the left	⊐	⊐
33	Move to the right	⊏	⊏
34	Place in the centre	Centre	⌐¬ indicating position
35	Raise line	Raise	
36	Lower line	Lower	
37	Straighten margin	‖	|
38	Passage omitted	Out see copy	λ
39	Remove printer's space	⊥	encircle space
40	Abbreviation or figure to be printed in full	Spell out	encircle words or figures

Fig 17 Correction signs

Credit card See **Banker's credit card** and **Telephone credit card**.

Credit note (business documents)   A credit note is sent from the seller to the buyer for one of the following reasons:
1   To credit a debtor with returns (returned goods).
2   To credit a debtor with an allowance or discount.
3   To credit a debtor to correct an overcharge on the invoice.
4   To credit a debtor when chargeable containers are returned.

Credit transaction   This is a transaction where payment for goods or services is not made at the time of purchase. See also **Cash transaction**.

Credit transfer system of the banks (current account)
The Bank Giro Credit Transfer System is a method of making multiple payments through the clearing banks.
By issuing one cheque a customer is able to have any number of amounts transferred. A good example of this is of a company paying salaries to its employees. All the payments are listed on a schedule showing the employees' bank branch code numbers, and a slip is made out for each one. The customer draws one cheque for the total amount. Slips, schedule and cheque are taken or posted to the company's own bank which sends the credits through the clearing system to the banks to which they are addressed. These salary credits are then credited to the payees' accounts on the second or third working day after being paid in.

Crossed cheques   If two parallel lines are drawn across the face of a cheque it must be paid into a bank account; this is a *general crossing*.

A/c payee only (Account payee only) appearing between the lines means that it can be paid only into the account of the payee. Occasionally the bank and branch of the payee's account are also clearly stated—this is known as a *special crossing*.

Cross-reference (filing) Sometimes correspondence or documents could be filed under more than one heading. In this case the most appropriate heading should be chosen, and a cross-reference put under the alternative heading, indicating where the information is kept.

Current account (banking) This is the most common account held by bank customers. To open a current account with a clearing bank a would-be account holder must comply with the following requirements of the bank:
1 He must deposit a sum of money.
2 He must furnish a personal reference, preferably from a customer.
3 He must give a specimen signature.
If the bank is satisfied the new customer will be given a personalised cheque book and personalised paying-in book (the latter made up of Bank Giro Credit slips). He will then be able to avail himself of the following current account services:

Paying-in money to a current account
a Paying-in slip (Bank Giro Credit Slip)
b Credit transfers (as payee)
c Direct debits (as payee)
d Standing orders (as payee)

Methods of payment through a current account
a Cheques (backed by a banker's cheque card if necessary)
b Banker's draft
c Credit transfers

Current account

d Standing orders
e Direct debits

Withdrawing cash from a current account
a Cheques (made payable to Cash) sometimes accompanied by a change/exchange form
b Cash dispenser card

Further facilities available to current account holders
a Bank statements
b Bank loan
c Bank overdraft
d Night-safe
Joint accounts and budget accounts are also available to current account customers.
Girobank also offers current account facilities, application forms for which are available at most post offices.

Paying-in money to a Girobank current account
a Transfer/deposit form

Methods of payment through Girobank
a Cheques backed by a Girobank cheque guarantee card
b Postcheque service
c Girobank payment services
d Standing orders
e Direct debit
f Transfer forms used to transfer money between Girobank accounts
g Transcash forms used to transfer money into a Girobank account by a non-Girobank customer

Further facilities available to Girobank customers
a Girobank statements of account
b Fixed interest personal loan
c Traveller's cheques and foreign currency through Thomas Cook

Curriculum vitae   This is a sketch of the course of one's life, and is a useful document to prepare for sending with applications for employment. At all times it should be kept completely up-to-date; it should list (chronologically where applicable):

Name   Date of birth   Sex   Marital status
Nationality
Home address and home telephone number
Schools, colleges and university attended, with dates
Qualifications obtained, with dates and grades
Past and present places of employment
Hobbies and interests
Names and addresses of two referees (from whom permission must be obtained before using their names).

Cursor (computers/word processors)   Movable mark on the screen that indicates where the next character will appear.

Cursor control keys (computers/word processors) Generally a set of four keys with arrows on them, indicating the way the cursor will move if the key is pressed.

Customs declaration form (overseas mail)   All packages for abroad are liable to be opened in the country of destination and the contents are subject to the customs and other legal requirements of that country; all such packages should be accompanied by a declaration form, details of which are available at post offices.

Cut-and-paste (word processors)   General name given to the task of moving pieces of text from one position to another.

D

In the Telephone Alphabet D is for David

Abbreviations

DD	direct debit
dept	department
disc	discount
div	division, dividend
do	ditto (Italian): repeat
dr	debtor, doctor

Daily stamp record (outgoing mail)   Also known as the **stamp book**. Though most firms use franking machines instead of adhesive stamps for outgoing mail, it is usual to keep some stamps for use in emergencies, etc. A record of such stamps is made in a stamp book which is usually kept on the Imprest system (qv), money for the purchase of stamps being obtained from petty cash.

Daisy wheel (typewriters/printers)   This is a single printing element which contains all the usual characters, each 'petal' of the daisy wheel holding a character of type. It can be changed and inserted easily to provide different typefaces, and the pitch can be changed by switching the selector.

Data (computers)   Any information given to a computer which will be worked on according to the instructions in a program. The information and results from a computer are also called DATA.

Database (computers)   An organised file of information held in the computer's memory, or on tape or disk.

Datapost (Royal Mail)   Datapost provides a fast, secure, highly reliable delivery service for urgent packages; it can be used both inland and internationally.

Data processing (computers)   The operation of collecting data, processing it, and presenting results. It can involve calculations required in making out the payroll of a firm, in stock control, and in general accountancy.

Datel (British Telecom)   British Telecom circuits provide rapid transmission, over telephones, telegraph or tele-printer lines, of information prepared in the forms suitable for computers (punched tape, etc).

Date order (filing)   Filing in the order of the date shown on the letter or document. Also known as chronological order.

Date stamp (incoming mail)   A piece of office equipment which stamps the day's date on incoming mail. A time-stamp is frequently incorporated in the date stamp, so that if a query should later arise the exact time of the docu-ment's delivery at the office will be known.

Dead file   When the subject in a file is no longer dealt with the file is 'dead' and is usually filed away from the main filing system. A record of such files is usually kept.

Debit note (transactions)   A debit note is similar to an invoice as it also tells the purchaser how much money he owes the supplier. It is used to make adjustments. For instance, if the supplier has undercharged on an invoice he will send a debit note for the difference. Also, freight and insurance charges not known at the time of the invoice can be charged by means of a debit note.

De-centralised filing This is the same as **departmental filing** and is the opposite of centralised filing. It is adopted by firms who find it more efficient if each department does its own filing, instead of sending all the filing to one central filing department. The advantages of departmental filing are that all the papers required are close at hand, and the staff involved are easily trained in the use of the system.

Decimal tab (word processors) A key used for entering numbers to ensure the alignment of the decimal point.

Decollator (office machinery) This machine, when coupled with an off-line guillotine, will separate duplicated sets of forms (continuous multipart stationery) into sets of individual forms. See fig 30.

Dedicated word processor A microcomputer which does only word processing.

Deductions from salaries and wages Before salaries or wages are paid to employees certain deductions are made. There are two types:
1 *Statutory deductions* These are compulsory by law. They are income tax (PAYE) and National Insurance.
2 *Voluntary deductions* These can include private medical insurance (eg BUPA), SAYE (Save as you earn), social clubs and welfare schemes, superannuation and union dues.

Deductions working sheet (P11—new) Income tax form supplied by the Inspector of Taxes for the employer to record the amount of income tax and national insurance contributions deducted from the employee's pay. There is a separate form for each employee. (See fig 31.)

Default (word processors) The name given to a value, such as a margin setting, which the word processor automatically assumes, in the absence of any other entry.

Delete (word processors)   To remove or eliminate a part of text, such as a word or a line. Text can also be deleted from a disk.

Delivery note (transactions)   This arrives with the goods and states what is being delivered at that particular time. It should be checked to see that there are no discrepancies. Often the delivery note is signed by the customer and returned to the vanman. Sometimes there is a copy for the customer to retain which also acts as an invoice or bill.

Departmental filing   Also known as **de-centralised filing**. In some companies it is more efficient if each department deals with its own filing, instead of sending all the filing to one central filing department. (See **Centralised filing**). The advantages of departmental filing are that the papers required are close at hand, and the staff involved are easily trained in the use of the system.

Deposit account (banking and girobank)   Money is left in a deposit account with the sole object of earning interest. Seven days' notice of withdrawal is required by the bank for withdrawals; withdrawals on demand are penalised by loss of interest money.

Descender (word processors/typewriters)   The part of a letter that appears below a baseline; eg the 'tails' of g, j, p, q, y.

Designation (business letters)   The position in a firm or organisation of the writer of a business letter. (Eg Works Manager, Sales Manager etc.)

Despatch Note (transactions)   Also known as an **advice note**. It tells the customer that his goods are being despatched from the warehouse or factory, and the method by which they are to be transported.

Dialling tone (telephone)   A low 'burr' which you should hear before you start to dial a number. If there is no tone the line is dead: report the matter at once to the Telecom engineers.

Diary   The most usual form of business diary for executives and their secretaries is the 'page-a-day' desk diary, which may be obtained with half- or quarter-hour times already printed. The bottom part of the page is often left blank for notes, and can be used for reminders.

It is usual for both executive and secretary to keep their own diaries, and it is essential that the secretary makes sure that all entries appear in both. This requires daily checking to avoid the possibility of double bookings; times of meetings should be entered as soon as they are known, even if the date is a long way ahead.

It is essential that an entry is made in the diary for every appointment or interview arranged, and in the diary (or some other follow-up system) of every matter requiring attention at a later date.

Dictating machines   These are used by audio-typists and are of two main types: those which use a magnetic medium, and those which use a non-magnetic medium. Magnetic media do not provide a permanent record, and all the media may be re-used (eg tapes). A permanent record can be made on non-magnetic media, such as discs. The advantages of dictating machines are:

1   Dictation can be given at any time the employer is free, leaving the typist free for other work.

2   Recording materials can often be sent through the post.

3   Work can be evenly distributed among the typists in a typing pool.

4   Because the amount of work can be measured management is enabled to increase output and efficiency.

Dictionary Book defining, in alphabetical order, the words of a language.

Dictionary (word processors)   A collection of short pieces of text, stored on disk, which is reserved for special applications; eg a disk-based spelling dictionary. Also called **library**.

Digital switchboard This has a microcomputer which provides for call queueing at busy periods, diverting unanswered calls to other extensions, the use of different ringing tones to distinguish outside calls from internal calls, and a memory store for numbers which are used frequently.

Direct bag (Royal Mail)   A large bag which is used for despatching several parcels to one address in the UK or abroad.

Direct debit (banking and Girobank)   This is a method of arranging for a bank to make periodic payments on behalf of its customer, and is a variation of the standing order system. It can be used for fixed amounts at fixed dates or for varying amounts at irregular intervals. A direct debit for an unspecified amount is called a variable amount direct debit.

With the direct debit system, instead of a company receiving payment of amounts due from its debtors under a standing order, the company requesting payment draws on the debtor's bank account. It claims the amount due for a period, eg month, week etc, from the bank. The company requesting payment will need its debtor's written authority before direct debiting can commence.

A big advantage of a direct debit over a standing order is that when a payment alters, perhaps owing to a change in Value Added Tax or a club simply wishing to raise its subscription, the increased amount is claimed and no action is required by the debtor, whereas with a standing order the bank would require a written instruction from its customer to make an increased payment. The banks take certain precautions to ensure that companies act responsibly in operating the system, and one of the conditions is that a company always notifies its debtors before an increased regular amount is claimed.

Most direct debit forms are now produced by the company requesting payment and are sent out as a detachable form which can be filled in and signed by the debtor and passed on to a clearing bank or Girobank, thus authorising payment.

Directory   Book with lists of inhabitants of districts, members of professions, etc, with various details.

Discount (transactions)   A discount is a reduction in a bill, given as a favour. There are three kinds of discount:

1 *Cash discount*   This is given to debtors who pay promptly for their goods when the time for payment arrives (eg $2\frac{1}{2}\%$ discount for payment within one month). Also known as **settlement discount**.

2 *Quantity discount*   Very often discount is given for large orders; the greater the quantity ordered the lower the unit cost.

3 *Trade discount*   This does not depend upon the time of payment, but is given by one trader to another trader. It is also the reduction in the catalogue price of an article, given by the wholesaler or manufacturer to the retailer to enable him to make a profit.

Discretionary hyphen (word processors)   A hyphen that is inserted between words to improve the appearance of text. A discretionary hyphen is not permanent: if the length of a line is changed, the hyphen may be automatically dropped by the system. See **Required hyphen**.

Disk (computers)   A storage device consisting of a flat circular plate, made of plastic or aluminium, coated with a magnetisable material. The disk may be exchangeable or fixed, floppy or hard.

Disk-drive (computers)   A device consisting of a motor and an electro-magnet which enables text to be stored on disks. The motor spins the disk while the recording head moves over the surface of the disk, recording text.

Display format (word processors)   The amount of characters that can fit on the screen, described as either the number of lines and characters per line, or the total number of characters.

Document (word processors)   A portion of text treated by the word processor as one complete unit.

Document assembly (word processors)   The procedure of collating separate sections of text, such as paragraphs, to form a new, complete document.

Documentation   Documents used in a business transaction.

Document destroying machine   Also known as a **shredder**. This shreds secret and confidential documents. Shredded paper is used to provide packing material for parcels.

Document recovery (word processors)   A facility on some word processors to re-establish a document which has been accidentally deleted.

Dot matrix (computers/printers)   Name given to a type of printer that prints characters as a set of fine dots within a grid of rows and columns, called a matrix.

Double time (salaries and wages)   This is time worked which is paid for at twice the basic rate, for instance Sunday or Bank Holiday work.

Draft   The first outline or rough copy of any document.

Drawee (cheque)   A cheque is said to be *drawn* on a bank, and the banker whose bank name and branch address appears at the top of a cheque is the drawee.

Drawer (cheque)   The drawer of a cheque is the person who signs the cheque authorising the bank to pay the money out. Unsigned cheques will not be honoured by the bank, even if the cheques are personalised, ie have the drawer's name printed on them by the bank.

Duplicate (computers)   To make a copy of either a document on a disk, or the contents of the whole disk, on to another disk.

Duplicating (reprographics)   The process which produces copies of a document from a specially prepared 'master'. The use of carbon and photocopiers now generally comes under the heading of 'duplicating'; sometimes the words 'replication' and 'reprographics' are used.

The centralised Reprographics Department of a large organisation will cover all aspects of duplicating. Spirit, ink (stencil) and offset-litho machines, photocopiers and collating machines will be housed in the department.

Office juniors are often employed in the Reprographics Department, where work coming in from different offices provides a good introduction to the work done by the whole organisation.

E

In the Telephone Alphabet E is for Edward

Abbreviations

ea	each
E & OE	errors and omissions excepted
EC	early closing
EEC	European Economic Community
EFT	electronic funds transfer
EFTA	European Free Trade Association
eg	*exempli gratia* (Latin): for example
enc(s)	enclosure(s)
esq	esquire
etc	*et cetera* (Latin): and the rest
et seq	*et sequens* (Latin): and the following
ex officio	(Latin): by virtue of his office
ext	extension

Earnings   This covers money earned in return for goods or services supplied by the self-employed, or salaries or wages paid to employees for specified services.

Edge-punched cards (filing)   Sometimes it is necessary to select from a number of index cards all those marked with the same information. A simple method is to punch the information on to the *edges* of the cards. To pick out all the cards with the same information a rod is inserted through the cards and all the cards with the same information will be collected together.

Edit (computers)   To rearrange text.

Electric Typewriter   This has two main advantages over the manual typewriter: it requires less energy from the typist and the type has an even impression.

Electronic filing systems   These involve the use of a micro-processor for quick retrieval of microfilm. VDU terminals are used to communicate directly with a computer which is able to locate a document filed on microfilm and displays the image of the required document on the screen.

Magnetic data storage methods such as tape, floppy disc etc, provide information in machine-readable format, and take up a fraction of the space required by conventional filing in filing cabinets. A more recent advance is the *digital optical recorder* which by using a laser beam allows the storage on disc of many pages of A4 text; any page can be accessed (located for viewing) within a quarter of a second.

Electronic funds transfer (computers)   A system of paying for goods by sending computer signals to change amounts in bank accounts. When paying for goods the customer inserts a plastic card into an electronic device connected to a computer of the retailer's bank. The customer keys in a personal identification number to debit his account and credit the retailer's account without the need for a cheque or any other paperwork.

Electronic mail (computers)   Electronic mail does not have to be posted in the normal way; it is transmitted electronically over telephone lines from one word processor to another which may be in another town or country. *Teletex* (operated by European postal authorities) provides the necessary services for communicating text by word processors at speeds of up to 3500 words per minute.

The Post Office *Electronic Post* service is now available for sending mass mailings by wire to be printed and enveloped in a distant centre for delivery through the post. The service uses a combination of computer transmission, laser printing and postal delivery, and is being run initially at London and Manchester. It is open to any firm with a computerised mailing list.

Electronic mailing equipment (outgoing mail)   The latest electronic franking machine has push-button controls for selecting postage values and can record the total value of postage used for individual batches of mail. An electronic franking machine can also be linked to electronic scales which automatically combine the weighing, postage calculation and franking operations. A remote meter-resetting system using a special telephone data pad enables additional units to be purchased and the franking machine reset by telephone without a post office having to be visited.

Electronic stencil scanner (duplicating)   This will produce facsimile stencils of original drawings or photographs for duplicating. The stencil is cut by an electronic stylus which produces a facsimile by travelling in lines across the original.

Electronic typewriter (See fig 18)   The Central Computer and Telecommunications Agency of HM Treasury produced in 1982 and published in 1983, for the Civil Service, a report on the use of Electronic Typewriters. These are their definitions of the different categories of machines:
Category A   This is a basic machine with an electronic keyboard, daisy wheel, choice of pitch and an automatic error correction from a small buffer memory. The buffer memory varies dependent upon the type of ELT and ranges from 15 characters to one line of type. The operator does not clear the memory because buffer memories clear

automatically by retaining only the last section of type. The basic ELTs have no internal/permanent memories and few facilities.

Fig 18 Electronic typewriter

Category B Machines in this category have 2–3 line correction buffer memories and also permanent memories of up to 4000 characters, plus automatic centring facilities, underlining and other features. There are few machines on the market with 1–4000 characters—most have less than 1000.

Category C These ELTs have internal/permanent memories larger than 4000 characters. Some of these ELTs do not have visual displays. Nevertheless they do have a wide range of automatic features, such as editing and storing facilities.

Category D Machines in this category have more varied features including unlimited external memories, eg, removable disks. (These can be interfaced with VDUs and upgraded to provide word-processing facilities.)

Electrostatic copiers (reprographics)   These are in general use today and can be divided into three main categories; high-speed plain-paper copiers; low- to medium-speed plain-paper copiers; and coated-paper copiers.

Elite type (typewriters)   A size of type which gives 12 characters to the inch (25 mm).

Emboldening (word processors)   A procedure whereby the word processor prints text in **bold** face—ie, in characters darker and thicker than normal.

Emergency tax card (P13)   An income-tax form which is used if an employee has no code number. When a code number is issued the record is transferred to the P11 Deductions Working Sheet.

Emulation (word processors)   An aspect of communications (qv) in which the word processor—to make the connection to another piece of equipment easier—'pretends' it is a common computer terminal.

Enclosure(s) (business letters)   Abbreviated *enc(s)*. Any form, printed matter, etc, which is enclosed with a letter is an enclosure. When an enclosure is sent, the fact is shown on the letter itself by adding the abbreviation *enc*, or plural *encs* at the bottom left-hand corner.

Endorsing (over) (cheques)   This is the signing of one's name on the back of a cheque, when the cheque is being paid into the account of a person who is not the named payee of the cheque.

Engaged tone (telephone)   This is a repeated single tone, and means that the called number or the British Telecom lines are in use.

Enquiry

Enquiry (business documents)   An enquiry can be sent on a special enquiry form or is sometimes sent in the form of a letter. Several likely suppliers are usually circulated by the prospective buyer.

Envelopes   These are available in a large variety of styles, and in a wide range of quality (weight), cutting and sealing.

POP envelopes (Post Office Preferred range)   The Post Office sorting machines are designed to take envelopes within a certain range of sizes. Envelopes (and cards) should be at least 90×140 mm, and not larger than 120×235 mm.

International envelope sizes are as follows:

	mm		mm
C3	324×458	B4	250×353
C4	229×324	B5	176×250
C5	162×229	B6/C4	125×324
C6	114×162	B6	125×176
C5/6 (DL)	110×220		
C7/6	81×162		
C7	81×114		

Types of envelope
aperture envelopes have cut-out panels through which the address written on the letter can be read. The panels are not covered with any protective material.
anti-trap envelopes have double flaps which prevent smaller items being entrapped when the envelope is sent un-sealed.
banker envelopes have the opening on the longer side.
pocket envelopes have the opening on the shorter side.
window envelopes have cut-out panels covered with trans-parent material through which the address written on the letter can be read.

Envelope-sealing machine (outgoing mail)   This moistens the gum and seals the flaps on envelopes. Envelopes are fed automatically into the machine, and the quick hygienic process enables large quantities of envelopes to be sealed securely. Some machines will frank mail at the same time.

ERNIE (Post Office)   This stands for Electronic Random Number Indicator Equipment—the complex machine which selects the numbers of winning Premium Bonds. Premium Savings Bonds are a government security. The only essential difference between them and other forms of small savings is that instead of earning interest the bonds carry, after a qualifying period, a chance of winning a tax-free prize.

Error detection (word processor)   A feature built into communications (qv) to ensure that any text sent to, or received from, another device has not been distorted during its transmission.

Estimate (transactions)   This is an estimated cost for particular goods or services and must be worked out for each enquirer.

eurocheque (current account)   Midland Bank is presently the only major UK clearing Bank to issue eurocheques to its current account customers. The cheques may be used at banks, hotels, shops and garages displaying the 'ec' sign and may be written in most European currencies to the guaranteed value of approximately £75.
The Midland eurocheque card may be used to withdraw money from over 500 cash-dispensing machines throughout Spain. On request, each card holder is given his/her own personal identification number. (See fig 19.)

eurocheque encashment card (current account)   This is issued to current account customers of British clearing banks other than Midland, for use while travelling abroad, as the cheque card used in the United Kingdom is no longer acceptable for the guaranteeing of cheques issued abroad.

Fig 19 Midland eurocheque card

Exchange disk (computers)   A disk that can be removed from the disk drive. Using interchangeable disks means that more than one disk can be used to store text. Floppy disks are exchangeable. See also **Fixed disks**.

Ex officio (meetings)   A Latin phrase meaning 'by virtue of his office'. An *ex officio* member of a committee is appointed to it because of some office he holds. For example, the head teacher of a school is often, by virtue of being the head teacher, the Chairman of the Parent/Teacher Committee.

Expresspost (Royal Mail special delivery)   This is a fast, same-day messenger collection and delivery service available in London and certain other large towns and cities. In addition to local services many same-day inter-city links between Expresspost centres are available.

Extension telephone   Abbreviated 'ext'. An internal telephone.

Extraordinary general meeting   In addition to the Annual General Meeting an Extraordinary General Meeting may be called at any time to discuss special business.

F

In the Telephone Alphabet F is for Frederick

Abbreviations

fas	free alongside ship
fob	free on board
fwd	forward

Face value   The value as stated on the face of a coin, note, share certificate etc. The nominal worth.

Facsimile   An exact copy.

Facsimile telegraphy (FAX—see fig 20)   Facsimile printer equipment can transmit any form of printed, typed or handwritten matter, drawings, diagrams and photographs from one location to another, at home or abroad, within a few minutes. Material can be transmitted over national and international telephone networks by the direct-dial system.

However, if customers have no facsimile machines of their own or have problems transmitting direct because of machine incompatibility or international time zone differences, use can be made of the Bureaufax service of British Telecom. Any black-and-white document up to A4 size can be sent to many countries overseas. Normally the document is transmitted by Bureaufax to similar bureaux abroad, who then arrange local delivery to the final destination.

Fig 20 Facsimile unit

Fanning Separating sheets of paper or card by running them rapidly through the fingers. Sometimes this is necessary before feeding paper into a duplicating machine.

Fibre ribbon (computers) A ribbon made of textile or nylon, and treated with ink. Its print quality is acceptable, it is inexpensive and it lasts a long time.

Field (computers) A subdivision of a record (qv) which contains only a specific type of information: eg in a 'name and address' record, the post code and town are both fields.

File (computers) An organised collection of related records on a disk etc; eg a set of names and addresses.

File reference The title shown on a file which identifies its position in the filing system. It can consist of any combination of letters or figures. Business letters often bear the file reference as a letter reference, which should be quoted on all outgoing and incoming correspondence dealing with the matter.

Filing (see also **Indexing**) A good filing system is essential to the smooth running of any firm or organisation, so that there is easy reference to any letter or document.
Some firms operate centralised filing departments; some decentralise and keep the filing in the separate departments, when it is known as departmental filing. For the five main filing systems see **alphabetical**, **chronological**, **geographical**, **numerical** and **subject filing.**

Filing hints:
1 Pre-sort all papers before filing so that the complete set is in order.
2 Remove paper clips, pins, and staples. Related papers should be stapled between the punch holes so that it is possible to refer to each sheet separately while it is in the file.
3 Always file new material on the top or front of the file. Any papers which have been borrowed and returned should be replaced in their correct order.

4 Never let a file become too overcrowded. If necessary start a new file (this is called a reserve or transfer file); if the old file is no longer required it may be filed in a 'reserve' drawer, but make sure that a note is put in the new file as to its whereabouts.

5 Make sure that the punch holes are parallel to the sides of the paper, so that when the papers are put in the file they will be straight.

6 Make sure that cross-references are used if papers could be filed under two separate headings.

Filing clerk   Filing is an office job usually given to juniors, but it is extremely important and papers improperly filed—and apparently 'lost'—can cause at the least annoyance and at the worst financial loss. Time spent in the Filing Department of a large firm is often part of a new employee's induction course as it will introduce a newcomer to all aspects of the organisation's sphere of work.

The most important part of a filing clerk's duties will, of course, consist of the filing away of all papers which have been dealt with; this will involve opening new files where necessary, cross-indexing, and in general keeping the filing system neat, tidy, and up-to-date. In a centralised Filing Department there will be a constant demand for files to be borrowed, and this will involve the use of outcards (also called outfolders); often the routing of documents with circulation slips (qv) will start from this department. There is usually a typewriter available for listing etc, so a filing clerk should be a reasonably good typist.

In a centralised filing department the young office worker will be in constant contact with other members of the organisation and should at all times be pleasant, courteous, and helpful.

Firm offer (business documents)   A firm offer is the quotation of a definite price for the goods or services mentioned, usually subject to a condition that it is accepted within a specified time. Such an offer can be withdrawn by the seller before it is accepted by the buyer, but it cannot be withdrawn after acceptance.

First-class letter post (Royal Mail)   This should be used for all urgent mail. Mail sent by this service will normally be delivered on the first working day after collection.

Fixed disk (computers)   A built-in disk which cannot be removed from the disk drive. One disk stores all the text. *cf* **exchangeable disk**.

Fixed-interest personal loans (Girobank)   Fixed-interest personal loans to assist the purchase of expensive items or home improvements may be granted to customers aged 18 or over.

Fixed time calls (British Telecom)   Trunk calls can be booked in advance for a particular time, but the time is not guaranteed. There is an extra charge for this service.

Flat file   A manila folder with a metal sliding clip which keeps the papers firmly in position.

Flexitime (salaries and wages)   Any system of flexible working hours in which a total of hours may be worked to suit the worker, often with the proviso that each day certain set hours (core times) are included.

Flexowriter (office machinery)   An electric typewriter of the automatic type which can punch holes in tape, read the tape and reproduce typewritten material from it. Letters and other business documents can therefore be produced from punched tape. The Flexowriter can complete this operation on one machine.

Flimsy (paper) (stationery)   A thin paper used for carbon copies.

Float   Money put into an account at its commencement. See **Imprest**.

Floppy disk (computers)   A small magnetic disk designed for use with microcomputer systems.

Flow chart (see fig 21)   Chart illustrating the nature and logical sequence of operations to be carried out, such as the movement of documents or the flow of work between individuals and departments.

Folding machine (outgoing mail)   This machine automatically folds documents, which are sometimes mailed without an outer cover.

Folio   A page in an account book.

Follow-up systems   Also known as **Bring forward systems**. In every office there must be some means of ensuring that matters requiring attention at a later date are not overlooked.

Because the office diary is a forecast of arrangements made for the future it is often used for this purpose. This is not very good office practice because—unless there is a special space reserved on each diary page (ie each day)—the notes can often overcrowd the pages and are not therefore very clear.

Follow-up systems can be used for various purposes. If, for example, the Sales Manager has been instructed to submit a fortnightly report to the Managing Director, then it would be the secretary's responsibility to bring this matter to his notice at the appropriate time. Reminders of the dates of meetings can be placed a few days earlier than the actual dates of the meetings.

Memory aids must be simple and easy to refer to. The following two methods are recommended:

1 *Card index reminder*   This is an index consisting of small cards, kept in a box or drawer. It is divided by twelve guide

Follow-up systems

Flow chart showing the movement of documents during a transaction
(No transaction would involve the use of *all* these documents)

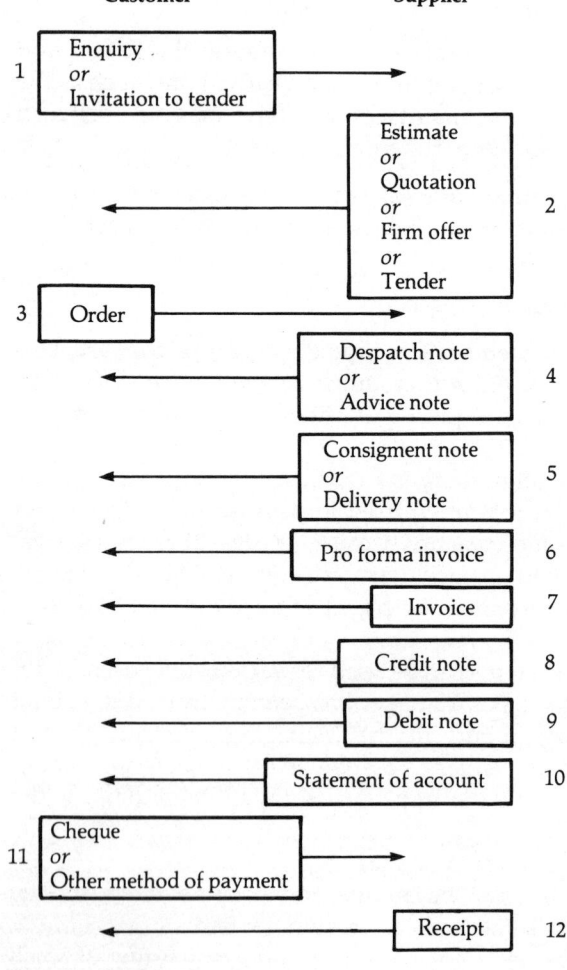

Fig 21 Flow chart

cards bearing the names of the months. Any matter requiring attention at a later date is indicated briefly on a card which is slipped behind the appropriate guide card *in order of date*. These cards must be referred to daily.

2 *Follow-up filing system* Instead of using a card index, divided by twelve cards bearing the names of the months, the 'follow-up' filing drawer contains twelve pockets marked January to December—the pocket for the current month containing a file which is subdivided into thirty-one number-indexed sections, one for each day of the month. Reminder cards or slips are filed in the appropriate monthly pocket, those for the current month being inserted in the appropriate daily slot. At the end of the current month these slips are removed and the file containing the daily inserts is used for the new current month. As with the card index these reminders must be referred to daily.

Font (computers)   A set of characters of a particular style and type, eg Pica Cubic.

Footer/footing (word processors)   A short piece of text or other information that appears at the bottom of every page in a document.

Footnote (word processors)   A piece of text which appears at the bottom of a page. It is referenced by a number, and elaborates on material contained within the main text. Do not confuse with **footer**.

Foreground (word processors)   A part of the word processor that handles text entry and editing, and any other activities which need the operator's direct involvement. *cf* **background**.

Foreign currency (banking and Girobank)   Foreign currency and traveller's cheques may be obtained by customers through clearing banks and Girobank. Girobank offers Thomas Cook Traveller's Cheques.

Foreign currency

Most banks will exchange foreign currency notes (but not small change) into British currency, providing the amount is not too large.

```
            HOMETOWN PRINTERS LTD
            HIGH STREET              HOMETOWN


    Your reference .............
    Date ......................


    Dear Sirs

    Thank you for your ................................

    dated ...........................................


    We hope to despatch the .........................

    in ..............................................


    Yours faithfully




    JOHN A SMITH
    Sales Manager
```

Fig 22 Form letter

Travellers abroad can also benefit from the use of a banker's credit card which may be used abroad for obtaining cash, paying hotel bills, etc. (See **eurocheque**).

Format (word processors)   The layout, presentation or arrangement of text on a screen or on paper.

Formatting (word processors)   The process of defining areas on a disk where text is to be stored. With some word processors the manufacturer's own brand of specially formatted disks must be used.

Form letters (see fig 22)   Form letters are used when the same message is sent to many addressees. It differs from a circular letter in that the information given in the letter has to be inserted each time a letter is sent to a different addressee. Sometimes cards are used for the same purpose.
Form letters are useful for sending the times and dates of interviews or appointments, for acknowledging receipt of letters, and for sending advice on the despatch of orders, etc.

Forms of address (correspondence)   It is important that the correct form of address is used in correspondence with persons of rank or title, both in the letter and on the envelope. Among the reference books containing this information are Black's *Titles and Forms of Address* and *Debrett's Peerage and Titles of Courtesy*.

Franking machine (outgoing mail)   (See fig 23) These help to speed and simplify the work of despatching the outgoing mail, as they print on the envelope or label any denomination of postage. They may be hired or purchased from companies licensed by the Royal Mail. Payment in respect of postage must be made in advance at a specified post office, and the meter on the machine will be set according to the amount prepaid. Most machines are clearly marked with a scale which records the balance in hand. Franking machines can also print an advertising slogan on envelopes. Hand and electric models are available and the latter also print gummed, franked labels ready to affix to packets or parcels. Whether the machines are used or not a *franking machine control card* must be completed weekly for the Royal Mail.

Fig 23 Franking machine

The latest electronic franking machine has push-button controls for selecting postage values and can record the total value of postage used for individual batches of mail. An electronic franking machine can also be linked to electronic scales which automatically combine the weighing, postage calculations and franking operations. A remote meter-resetting system using a special telephone data pad enables additional units to be purchased and the franking machine reset by telephone without having to visit a post office.

Freefone (British Telecom)   This service enables customers, clients, agents or employees to telephone an organisation without cost to themselves.

Freepost (Royal Mail)   This service enables customers, clients, agents or employees to mail letters (second class only) to an organisation without cost to themselves, the word FREEPOST appearing in the address.

This service can be used to attract a response to advertising not only in the press, but through television and direct mail. The postage plus a small fee on each item is paid by the addressee.

Function keys (word processors)   Extra keys found only on a word processor keyboard. They are used to control editing, printing, storage and other processing of text.

G

In the Telephone Alphabet G is for George

Abbreviations

GATT	General Agreement on Tariffs and Trade
Glos	Gloucester
GMT	Greenwich Mean Time

Gazetteer   A geographical dictionary; an alphabetical list of places.

Geographical filing   One of the five main filing systems. It is used by firms that employ sales representatives, agents or travellers, or in any system where it is necessary to divide the country into different areas or counties. Whatever is filed under the main areas—towns, names of agents, names of customers, or districts—is again filed alphabetically, as are the main areas.

Girobank   The national banking system operated from post offices and offering a competitive service with that of the clearing banks. It enjoys no special privileges and has to compete in the market place with other banks.
Girobank offers its customers current, deposit and budget account facilities.
Payment of money *into* a Girobank current account is made by means of a transfer deposit form.
Further facilities available to Girobank customers are fixed

90

interest personal loans, and traveller's cheques and foreign currency through Thomas Cook.

Girobank business accounts directory A directory of all businesses which have Girobank accounts, with their Girobank numbers.

Fig 24 Girobank standard cheque

Girobank cheques (see fig 24) *Cashing a cheque* An account holder's cheque made payable to Self can be cashed at a post office. Account holders with a *Girobank standard card* may cash a cheque for up to £50 every other working day at either of two post offices named on the card. If an account holder wishes to draw more than £50, or requires cash from a post office not named on his card, he must first send the cheque to Girobank at Bootle (postage is free). The cheque will be returned after the account has been debited and can then be cashed at a post office.

Paying by cheque The person or organisation receiving a Girobank cheque must arrange for it to be paid into a bank. If the payee wishes to receive the cheque payment in cash the cheque must first be sent to Bootle for authentication; it will be returned to the payee who may then cash it at a post office.

Girobank cheque guarantee card This enables the holder to cash a cheque for up to £100 every other working day at the post office named on the card or up to £50 every other working day at any post office transacting Girobank business. In addition this card can be used to guarantee payments up to £50.

Girobank methods of payment The following methods of payment are available to Girobank customers: banker's draft, direct debit, Girobank Payment Services, Girobank cheques (if necessary backed by a Girobank cheque guarantee card), standing order, and Transfer (between Girobank accounts).

Girobank payment services This is comparable to the Bank Giro Credit System of the banks, and like it is used in the payment of salaries, wages and occupational pensions, provided that employees are willing to open Giro accounts. The money is credited to the account of the employee automatically, the employee receiving only a pay advice giving the details of his earnings and deductions, and the amount transferred to his account.

Girobank postcheques See fig 25. A Girobank cheque service which enables guarantee card holders to withdraw money from their Girobank account at over 88 000 post offices in 28 countries in Europe and North Africa.

Girobank standard card This is *not* a cheque guarantee or credit card. It may only be used by account holders to cash cheques at the two post offices named on it.

Girobank statement of account See fig 26. This is the equivalent of the clearing banks' bank statement. It is sent,

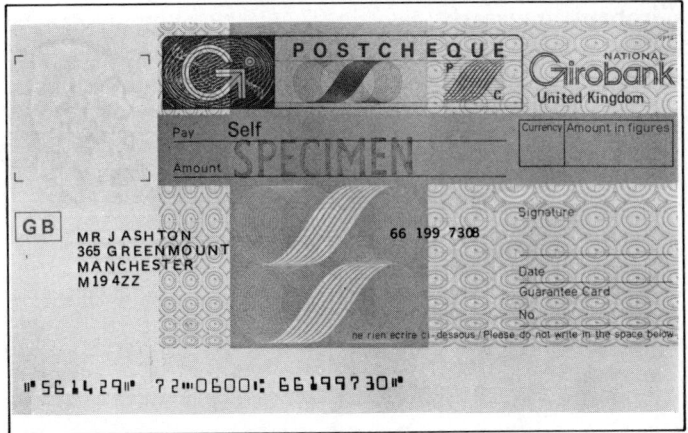

Fig 25 Girobank postcheque

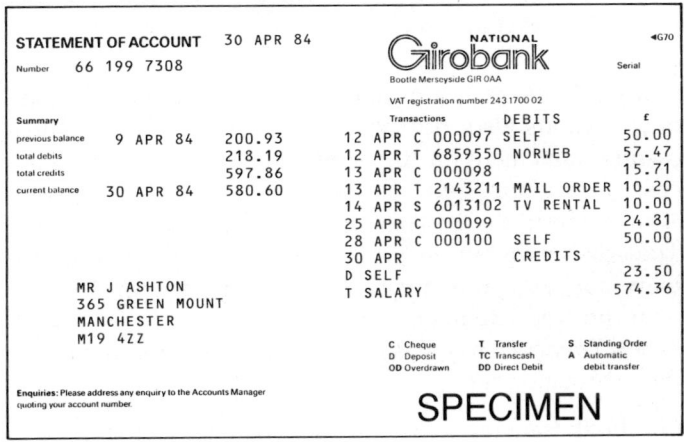

Fig 26 Girobank statement of account

free of charge, to an account holder every time a payment is made into his account, or after there have been 10 payments out since the last statement. Girobank statements of account are sent daily to all businesses.

Girobank transcash See fig 27. Cash payments can be made at post offices to people and organisations with Girobank accounts *by persons without Girobank accounts.*

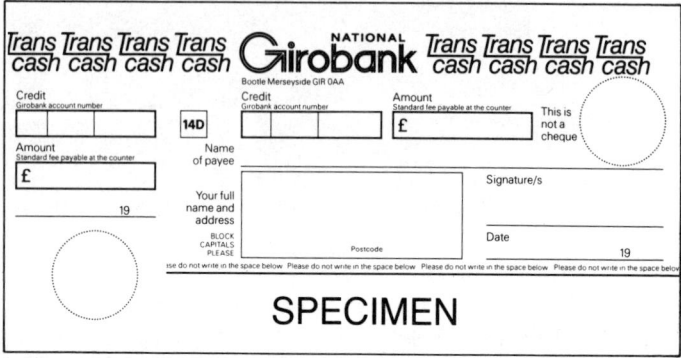

Fig 27 Girobank transcash form

Transcash forms are available at post offices and many organisations also incorporate them in their bills. Transcash is convenient for the payment of bills as it avoids the cost of envelopes and postage, though a fee is charged.

A message to the payee may be written on the back of a Transcash form but the post office will not accept responsibility for the authenticity of any message or for any unauthorised alteration of it.

When *Transcash freepay* is used, the *payee* organisation pays the transaction fee.

Girobank transfer/deposit forms See figs 28 and 29. This is used by Girobank current account customers for:

1 Paying *cash* into their own account at a post office.

2 Paying *cheques* into their own account. Cheques may not be deposited at a post office but must be sent direct to National Girobank at Bootle, with a completed transfer/deposit form.

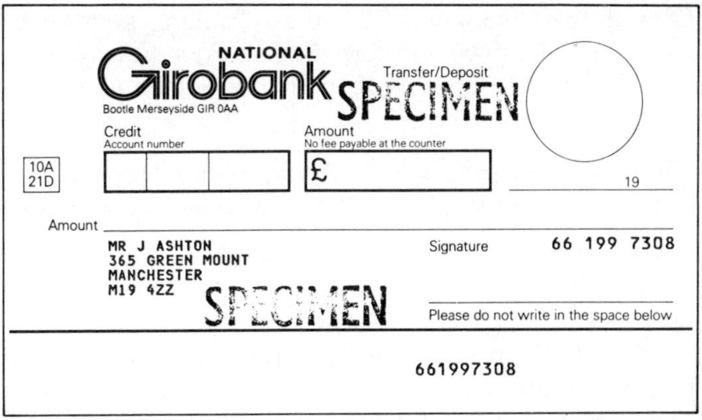

NATIONAL Girobank Transfer/Deposit SPECIMEN
Bootle Merseyside GIR 0AA
Credit
Account number
Amount
No fee payable at the counter
£
10A
21D
19
Amount
MR J ASHTON
365 GREEN MOUNT
MANCHESTER
M19 4ZZ
SPECIMEN
Signature
66 199 7308
Please do not write in the space below
661997308

Fig 28 Girobank transfer/deposit form

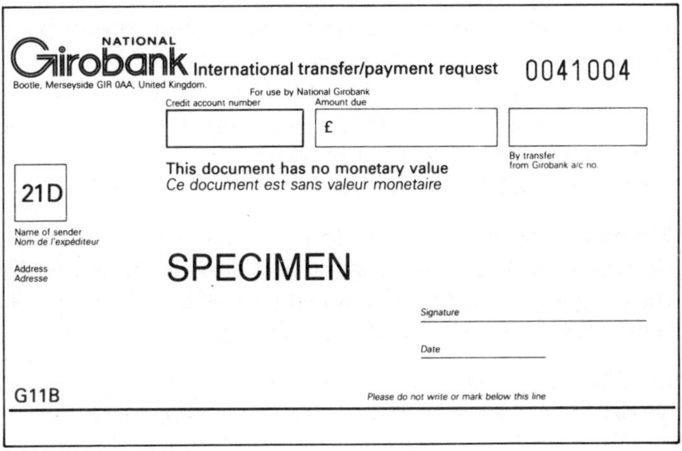

NATIONAL Girobank International transfer/payment request 0041004
Bootle, Merseyside GIR 0AA, United Kingdom.
For use by National Girobank
Credit account number
Amount due
£
By transfer from Girobank a/c no.
This document has no monetary value
Ce document est sans valeur monetaire
21D
Name of sender
Nom de l'expéditeur
Address
Adresse
SPECIMEN
Signature
Date
G11B
Please do not write or mark below this line

Fig 29 Girobank international transfer form

3 Transferring money from one Girobank account to another Girobank account.
4 An International Transfer Form is used for making payments overseas.

Giro systems (banking) These are banking systems by which money can be transferred direct from the account of one account holder to that of another person (or to those of more than one person).

Glossary (word processors) A term used by some manufacturers to describe a collection of standard paragraphs.

'Golf ball' typewriter This has a single printing element containing all the usual characters. When the keys are operated the 'golf ball', not the carriage, moves and is revolved to the printing point required. The 'golf ball' can be removed and a new one of a different type style inserted easily, making it useful for typing documents where a variety of type styles and sizes are required.

Goods received note (transactions) When goods have been received by an organisation a goods received note is made out in triplicate. One is sent to the Accounts Department for checking the invoice; one goes to the stores for entering the receipt on their records; the third is sent to the department which ordered the goods.

Graphics pad (computers) Information, such as technical drawings and graphs, can be put into a computer by drawing on a magnetically sensitive surface with a special pen. This surface is called a graphics pad.

Graphs Both bar graphs and line graphs are used in offices for the visual presentation of statistical data.

Green label letters (Royal Mail) Green labels (either adhesive or tie-on) stating contents and value must be affixed to all small packets and letters containing goods for addresses abroad, whether the goods are dutiable or not.

Gross pay (salaries and wages) The full amount of salaries or wages before any deductions have been made.

Guide cards (filing and indexing) These are inserted among index cards, or files, to make it easier to find the right information. They are often a different colour from the ordinary cards, and have a tab at the top on which is written the nature of the information which follows. Primary guide cards indicate the main filing divisions (eg A, B, C, D etc). Secondary guide cards indicate sub-divisions—Aa, Ab, Ac etc.

Fig 30 Guillotine/decollator

Guillotine (office equipment) A razor-sharp cutting device used for slicing quantities of paper and cardboard to the required size and for straightening tattered or uneven edges of paper.

Guillotine and decollator (office machinery) See fig 30. The latest off-line guillotines and decollators have been designed to meet the continuous stationery requirements of the computer operation. This new equipment helps to speed the flow of documents from the computer printer right through to final distribution. The cutting system removes any trace of perforations on standard computer forms, and sprocket holes can also be neatly removed to produce documents with a professional appearance. Following trimming, the decollator will separate duplicated sets of forms (continuous multipart stationery) into sets of individual forms. In addition, carbon rewind spindles are also available when the user requires removal of the carbon interleaf.

H

In the Telephone Alphabet H is for Harry

Abbreviations

Hants	Hampshire
HMSO	Her Majesty's Stationery Office
Hon Sec.	Honorary Secretary
HP	hire purchase
HQ	headquarters
hrs	hours

Hard disk (computers)   A disk which is made of rigid material, such as aluminium. Hard disks may be fixed or exchangeable.

Hardware (computers)   All the computer equipment, including the computer itself, input and output equipment, and magnetic disk and tape equipment (*cf* **software**).

Headed paper (business letters)   Headed paper is usually bond paper of superior quality. All or some of the following information is printed on it:
 1 Name of firm or organisation
 2 Address of firm
 3 Nature of business (ie Printers, Stationers, Civil Engineers etc)
 4 Telephone number (prefixed by STD code)
 5 Telex number
 6 Your reference (for the file reference of the addressee)

7 Our reference (for the file reference of the writer)
8 VAT registered number
9 Girobank customer account number (to facilitate any payments to the firm the addressee may require to make)
10 Telegraphic name and address (an addressing code approved by British Telecom)

Limited companies only—Address of registered offices
Names of directors and their countries of origin

Header/heading (word processors)   A short piece of text or other information that appears at the top of every page in a document.

Health and safety at work   Employers have a legal duty under the law to take reasonable care of their employees and provide a safe system of working. Employees should also take all reasonable care especially in the use of equipment.
The Offices, Shops and Railway Premises Act 1963 covers regulations dealing with the provision of suitable sanitary accommodation, satisfactory standards of cleanliness, ventilation, lighting and heating, the avoidance of overcrowding, fire prevention precautions, safety of office machinery.
The Health and Safety at Work Act 1974 covers everyone at work, and also increases the protection of the general public from industrial hazards. This Act sets out certain mimimum standards of safety, health and welfare.

Hectograph carbons (spirit duplicating)   Also known as **transfer sheet**. This is used in the preparation of spirit masters; the coated side is placed against the glossy side of special master paper. By typing (or writing) upon the master a reverse impression of the matter to be duplicated is transferred to the back of the master.

Hologram (computers)   A photographic system which uses laser light to create a three-dimensional image.

Home (word processors)   Name given to the top left-hand side of the screen.

Horizontal filing   Also known as **flat** or **plan filing**. Cabinets with shallow drawers can be used to keep large plans or pictures flat and protected.

Hot zone (word processors)   Also called **soft zone**. An area in a line of text to the left of the right margin, of adjustable size. The word processor detects any word that starts in the hot zone, and if the word will not fit on the line, a hyphen can be inserted. Hot zones are used to tidy up the appearance of text which has been created with word *wraparound*.

Household delivery service (Royal Mail)   This service provides for door-to-door delivery of unaddressed items to every address in a specified area. The smallest area for delivery will be a postman's 'walk'. Items need not be enveloped and no stamps are required.

Hyphenation (word processors)   The division of a word into two parts if it cannot fit on one line. The first part of the word is ended with a hyphen.

I

In the Telephone Alphabet I is for Isaac

Abbreviations

IDD	International Direct Dialling
ie	*id est* (Latin) that is
I/F	insufficient funds
inc	increase; incorporated
inf info }	information
ins	inches; insurance
int	interest; interim
inv	invoice
IOU	I owe you
ital	italics

Imprest   The amount of the float in the imprest system of accounting (qv).

Imprest system (petty cash)   A common procedure is to hand to the petty cashier a cheque for the first sum sufficient to cover the usual Petty Cash expenditure for a week or a month. On the petty cash book being checked and posted the petty cashier is reimbursed for the amount expended during the period. He therefore starts the next period with the same sum as the one with which he started the last.

Income tax   This is a statutory deduction from salaries and wages, and is a tax on earnings levied for meeting the expenses of the government. It is deducted on the government's behalf by employers from employees' salaries and wages at the time of payment, and is therefore known as PAYE (Pay As You Earn).

The amount of income tax deducted by the employer each pay-day depends on the employee's code number, which represents the amount of 'free pay' (ie that part of his income which is *not* taxed) to which he is entitled. The 'free pay' is ascertained by reference to tax table 'A', and the figure obtained deducted from the employee's gross pay. Tax is payable on this figure which is then referred to in tax table 'B', where the correct amount of income tax payable will be shown for the particular week or month.

Income tax forms   The following forms are the most familiar:

P6 Notice of Amended Coding   This is sent by the Collector of Taxes to an employer when the tax code number of an employee has been changed.

P11 (New) Deductions Working Sheet   This is supplied by the Inspector of Taxes for the employer to record the amount of income tax and National Insurance contributions deducted from the employee's pay. There is a separate form for each employee. (See fig 31).

P13 Emergency Tax Card   This card is used if an employee has no code number. When a code number is issued the record is transferred to the P11.

P14 End of Year Return   An income tax form made out in triplicate at the end of each year by employers for each employee. The top copy is sent to the Collector of Taxes for the Department of Health and Social Security; the second copy is sent to the Collector of Taxes for the Inland Revenue; *the third copy is the P60 Certificate of pay, tax deducted and National Insurance contributions*, and is given to each employee as proof that his income

Income tax forms

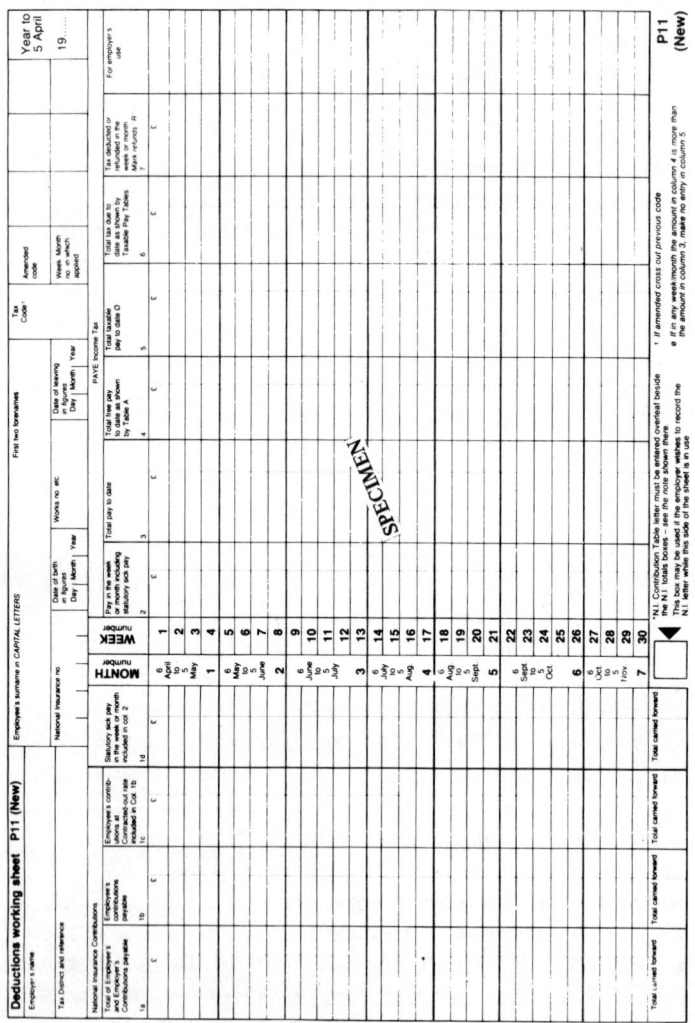

Fig 31 Income tax form P11 (*Crown copyright*)

tax and NI contributions have been paid for the year shown.

P15 Coding Claim This will be given to an employee who has no code number, possibly because he cannot get a P45 or has lost it, or because he is earning money for the first time. (See fig 32)

P15 CODING CLAIM

Tax reference

Please read these notes carefully before filling in this form:

Your new employer has given you this form because you have not given him a form P45. Without a P45 you may pay the wrong amount of tax.

- If you have left a job recently, contact your old employer and try to get a P45.
- If you expect to be able to give a P45 to your new employer in the near future, you need not fill in this form.
- If you cannot get a P45, or you have lost it, fill in this form and send it to the tax office in the envelope provided.
- If this is your first paid job, fill in this form and send it to the tax office in the envelope provided.

This form will help to give you a correct PAYE code so that you pay the right tax. You may not have to fill in all of it. Please follow the instructions in blue and fill in those sections that apply to you, using BLOCK CAPITALS.

A **Everyone should fill in this section:**

Your surname .... Mr/Mrs/Miss/Ms ....

Your Christian names or first names ....

The name and address of your new employer ....

SPECIMEN

....

The title or description of your new job .... Your National Insurance number

Is this new job your **only** job? If you have a second job, or do part-time or evening work, any payments you receive are part of your income. They are taxable in just the same way as the earnings from your regular job.

Please say YES or NO ....

If your answer is 'YES', please turn to page 2. If your answer is 'NO', please fill in section B below.

B Please give details of **any other work** for which you get paid:

The title or description of the job .... If you work for yourself please write 'self-employed' ....

The name and address of the employer ....

....

Your works or check number (if any) .... The branch or site where you work ....

The tax reference (if known) .... Your total weekly earnings from the work before any stoppages £ ....

Which is your **main** job? Is it your new job, shown in section A? Or the job shown in section B?

Please write A or B ....

If your answer is 'A', please turn to page 2.

If your answer is 'B', please turn straight to page 4: there is no need to fill in pages 2 and 3.

Page 1

Fig 32 Income tax form P15 (*Crown copyright*)

P45 Particulars of Employee Leaving When an employee leaves one place of employment for another the employee is given a form P45 on which is written the total taxable pay to date and the total tax deducted to date.

P45

Details of EMPLOYEE LEAVING

PART 1

		District number	Reference number
1.	PAYE reference		

2.	National Insurance number

			Mr. Mrs. Miss
3.	Surname *(Use BLOCK letters)*		
	First two forenames *(Use BLOCK letters)*		

		Day	Month	Year
4.	Date of leaving *(in figures)*			19

			Code	Week 1 or Month 1
5.	Code at date of leaving *If Week 1 or Month 1 basis applies, please also write "X" in the box marked "Week 1 or Month 1"*			

			Week	Month
6.	Last entries on Deduction Card *If Week 1 or Month 1 basis applies, complete item 7 instead*	Week or Month number		
		Total pay to date	£	p
		Total tax to date	£	p

7.	Week 1 or Month 1 basis applies	Total pay in this employment	£ p
		Total tax in this employment	£ p

SPECIMEN

8.	Works number		9. Branch, Contract Department, etc.

10.	Employee's private address	.... Postcode.....................

11. I certify that the details entered at items 1 to 9 above are correct.

Employer

Address

Date   Postcode

INSTRUCTIONS TO EMPLOYER

For Tax Office use

- Complete this form according to the "Employee leaving" instructions on the P8 (BLUE CARD).
- Detach Part 1 and send it to your Tax Office **IMMEDIATELY.**
- Hand Parts 2 and 3 (unseparated) to your employee **WHEN HE LEAVES.**
- IF THE EMPLOYEE HAS DIED, please write "D" in this box and send ALL THREE PARTS of this form (unseparated) to your Tax Office **IMMEDIATELY.**

For Centre use		
Amended	M/E	P

P45   HPB 1166 5/80

Fig 33 Income tax form P45 (*Crown copyright*)

One copy is sent to the employer's tax office, and two are given to the employee to give to his new employer, who keeps one and sends the other to the employee's new tax office. (See fig 33)

P46 Particulars of First Employment Form sent by the employer of a person earning money for the first time, to the Inspector of Taxes.

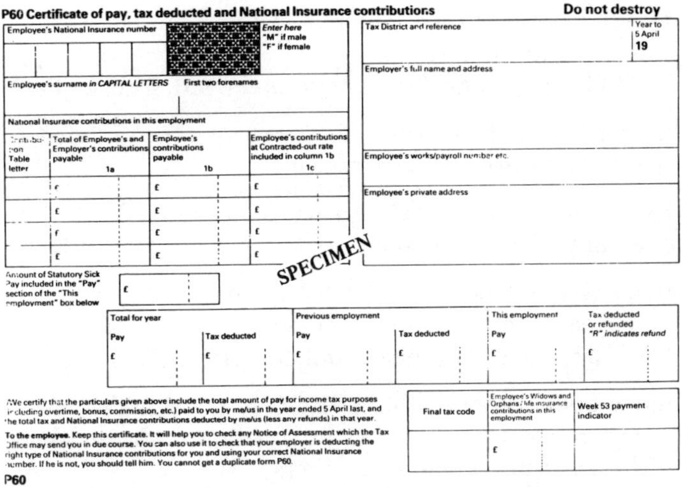

P60 Certificate of pay, tax deducted and National Insurance contributions **Do not destroy**

Employee's National Insurance number | *Enter here* "M" if male "F" if female

Tax District and reference | Year to 5 April 19

Employer's full name and address

Employee's surname *in CAPITAL LETTERS* | First two forenames

National Insurance contributions in this employment

Contribution Table letter	Total of Employee's and Employer's contributions payable 1a	Employee's contributions payable 1b	Employee's contributions at Contracted-out rate included in column 1b 1c
	£	£	£
	£	£	£
	£	£	£
	£	£	£

Employee's works/payroll number etc.

Employee's private address

SPECIMEN

Amount of Statutory Sick Pay included in the "Pay" section of the "This employment" box below £

Total for year: Pay	Total for year: Tax deducted	Previous employment: Pay	Previous employment: Tax deducted	This employment: Pay	Tax deducted or refunded *"R" indicates refund*
£	£	£	£	£	£

I/We certify that the particulars given above include the total amount of pay for income tax purposes (including overtime, bonus, commission, etc.) paid to you by me/us in the year ended 5 April last, and the total tax and National Insurance contributions deducted by me/us (less any refunds) in that year.

To the employee. Keep this certificate. It will help you to check any Notice of Assessment which the Tax Office may send you in due course. You can also use it to check that your employer is deducting the right type of National Insurance contributions for you and using your correct National Insurance number. If he is not, you should tell him. You cannot get a duplicate form P60.

Final tax code	Employee's Widows and Orphans / life insurance contributions in this employment	Week 53 payment indicator
	£	

P60

Fig 34 Income tax form P60 (*Crown copyright*)

P60 Certificate of Pay, Tax Deducted and National Insurance Contributions This is the third copy of the P14 which is made out annually by employers for each employee. It is proof that income tax and National Insurance contributions have been paid for the year shown. This is an important document and should be carefully kept; *duplicates cannot be obtained*. (See fig 34)

Incoming mail (mailing room) In a large organisation all mail is handled in a centralised mailing room, where the incoming mail is received and distributed to the departments concerned.

1 Letters are opened by a letter-opening machine except for those marked Confidential or Personal, which are delivered to addressees unopened.

2 Letters are date-stamped.

3 Registered mail and Recorded Delivery mail are recorded separately.

4 All remittances are entered in the Remittances Book and taken to the cashier.

5 Mail is sorted by departments and distributed to them.

Indent (word processors)   To start text entry a number of spaces away from the left margin.

Index   An alphabetical register of subjects dealt with, often at the end of a book.

Index (word processors)   A list of documents, automatically created by the word processor, that are held on disk. The index shows the name and size of each document.

Index book   Book with the letters of the alphabet visible in order, used for entering information such as names, addresses and telephone numbers.

Indexing   An index should provide a quick means of locating information and is therefore an essential part of most office filing systems.

Index-linked (pensions and savings) Index-linking means adjusting the interest on investments, or the amount paid out as pension, so that the money eventually received will be worth roughly as much in goods and services as it would have been at the time of the original investment, even if prices have changed in the meantime. In fact, even if RPI falls, the amount returned to the index-linked saver is never less than the total contributions he has made. This change in prices is measured by the UK General Index of Retail Prices (RPI). See also **Retail price index**.

Ink (stencil) duplicating   This is an excellent method of producing a large number of copies of circular letters, reports, minutes of meetings, agendas, menus, house magazines, instruction manuals etc.

Required for the production of masters—
  a prepared stencil
  correcting fluid and a ruler for passing beneath the stencil when using it.
  a *stylus* pen if any hand-written matter is required.
NB Before typing a stencil the type must be clean and the ribbon switched off. Masters can be produced also by photographic and electronic processes; the electronic scanner and photocopiers can produce a facsimile stencil of an original drawing or photograph for duplicating. Though stencil duplicating can be used for work in several colours the process is time-consuming and not always successful.

Required for producing copies on an ink duplicator—
  semi-sorb paper
  ink of the required colour.

Advantage of ink (stencil) duplicating:
1 Large numbers of copies can be reproduced (up to 5000)
2 Good quality reproduction is achieved
3 Stencils can be stored and re-used
4 The copy paper is cheap
5 The machine is easy to operate

Disadvantages of ink (stencil) duplicating:
1 The absorbent paper is unsatisfactory for handwriting.
2 Two or more colours require two or more separate runs.
3 For a few copies it can be expensive.

In/out board (reception)   This may be used at the Reception Desk to indicate which executives are on the premises.

Input (computers)   The most common method used in offices to input data is by way of a keyboard connected to a terminal and linked to the computer. Other methods include: *OMR* (optical marks as on multiple choice examination answers); *OCR* (optical character recognition where specially shaped characters can be recognised by the computer equipment; *MICR* (magnetic ink character recognition as used on cheques; *bar codes* as at supermarket point of sales.

Insert (word processors)   To add characters, lines or other portions of text to existing text.

Inserting and mailing machines (outgoing mail)   These collate up to eight enclosures, open the envelopes' flaps and insert the enclosures; moisten the flaps, seal the envelopes; print a postal impression on the envelopes, and count and stack the envelopes.

Insufficient funds (Abbreviated **I/F**) (cheques)   Cheques marked I/F, when returned to the payee, indicate that there was not enough money in the drawer's account to pay the amount shown. The payee should contact the drawer.

Intelpost (Royal Mail special service)   This is a facsimile transmission service offering high quality black and white reproduction of documents up to A4 size. Urgent letters and documents may be transmitted for same-day delivery between certain major centres in the United Kingdom and overseas.

Interest   This must be paid by the borrower on bank loans, overdrafts etc. The interest rate is displayed in all banks. Most hire purchase involves payment of interest. Interest is also paid *to* investors on all moneys they invest.

Interface (word processors)   An aspect of communications, being the physical connection between (for example) a word processor and another device. The interface arranges text and controls the transmission of text between the machines.

Internal   Within the same firm or organisation.

Internal memorandum (Abbreviated **memo**) (communications)   Both memoranda and memorandums are acceptable plurals. This is a form used for internal letters, messages and reports between departments on one site, to and from branch offices, and to representatives or agents in other parts of the country. No salutation or complimentary close is used.

Internal methods of communication   These are methods used for all types of communication within the same firm or organisation. They include the use of *memoranda, message pads, messengers, circulation slips, paging* and *public address systems, internal telephone systems, confravision, teleconferencing* and *teleprinters*.

Internal telephone systems   There are three main systems:
1   An internal telephone system (*PAX*—Private Automatic Exchange), entirely separate from the public exchange system, allows users to contact one another quickly. It has press-button operation and is available in three sizes.
2   *Manual switchboards* (*PMBX*—Private Manual Branch Exchange). There are two types: table-top switchboards in a variety of sizes, the largest of which has capacity for up to 10 exchange lines and 48 extensions; and floor-standing switchboards for use where a large capacity is required.

111

3 *Automatic switchboards* (*PABX*—Private Automatic Branch Exchange). A wide range of automatic installations is available. These combine exchange line service and intercom facilities in one telephone. The facilities provided offer many benefits, such as direct dialling of exchange line calls and extension-to-extension dialling, which reduce operating work to a minimum. With these systems the operator is able to give maximum attention and service to incoming callers.

Digital switchboards have a microcomputer which provides for call queueing at busy periods, diverting unanswered calls to other extensions, the use of different ringing tones to distinguish outside calls from internal calls, and a memory store for numbers which are used frequently.

International direct dialling (British Telecom) Abbreviated IDD   This facility enables subscribers in the United Kingdom to dial direct to many places overseas.

International paper sizes (stationery)   The 'A' Series:

A1	594 × 841 mm	Large sheets for plans and art work
A2	420 × 594 mm	
A3	297 × 420 mm	Legal documents, charts, plans and posters
A4	210 × 297 mm	Letters (business and official), legal and technical work, reports, minutes, agendas, literary work
*A5	148 × 210 mm	Letters (short business and official), inter-departmental correspondence (memoranda), actors' parts

*A5 paper when used with the shorter edge at the top is known as *portrait*

A5 paper when used with the longer edge at the top is known as *landscape*

A6	105 × 148 mm	Message pads, petty cash vouchers, requisitions, acknowledgment cards

| A7 | 74 × 105 mm | Compliment slips, circulation slips, receipts |
| A8 | 52 × 74 mm | Visiting cards |

International payments service (Post Office)   Internationalal payments may be sent to all countries, subject to compliance with any special conditions imposed by the country of destination. The form 'Sending Money Abroad' should be used; the full details requested on the form should be completed in block capitals. There is no limit to the amount of money that may be sent abroad, but the service is subject to a handling charge. The most expeditious means of transmission will be used, but no guarantee of a delivery time can be given.

International reply coupons (See fig 52)   It is not possible to send a stamped and addressed envelope to anyone abroad or in the Commonwealth. Reply coupons may be bought at the post office and should be enclosed with the letter requiring a reply, together with an addressed envelope. The addressee can then exchange his Reply Coupon at a post office for the appropriate stamps of his own country, which he then affixes to the envelope.

Inventory   A list of stock or equipment; a catalogue.
An *annual inventory* is the annual stock count which involves stocktaking of furniture, equipment, fixtures and fittings and is usually made in addition to the annual stocktaking of items in the stockrooms. It is needed for accounting purposes, and the information is also useful when it comes to assessing the amount of insurance cover needed by the firm against fire and theft.
A *perpetual inventory* goes on throughout the year, and allows for the process to be incorporated in the normal running of the stockroom. It is particularly useful where the stock items are fast-moving.

Invitations

Invitations (formal) and **replies to invitations** Formal invitations and replies to them are written in the third

```
            Mr and Mrs R Browning

      request the pleasure of the company of

      ....................................

      at the marriage of their daughter, Diana

               to Mr Philip Gardiner

              at St John's Church, Bath

          on Saturday, 21 March 19-- at 12 noon

           and afterwards at the Regal Hotel

      26 Regency Court
      BATH   BA3 4CX                        RSVP
```

Fig 35 Formal invitation

person. No salutation, subscription or signature is required. Fig 35 is an example of a formal invitation. An appropriate reply, to an invitation, which should be on headed paper and dated, might be as follows:

Formal acceptance Mr and Mrs Peter Brown thank Mr and Mrs John Smith for their kind invitation to a House-warming to be held at 8 The Close, Bridgetown on Friday, 20 June at 7.00 pm, and have much pleasure in accepting.

Formal refusal Mr and Mrs Peter Brown thank Mr and Mrs John Smith for their kind invitation to a House-warming to be held at 8 The Close, Bridgetown on Friday, 20 June at 7.00 pm.

They regret, however, that owing to a previous engagement they must decline the invitation.

114

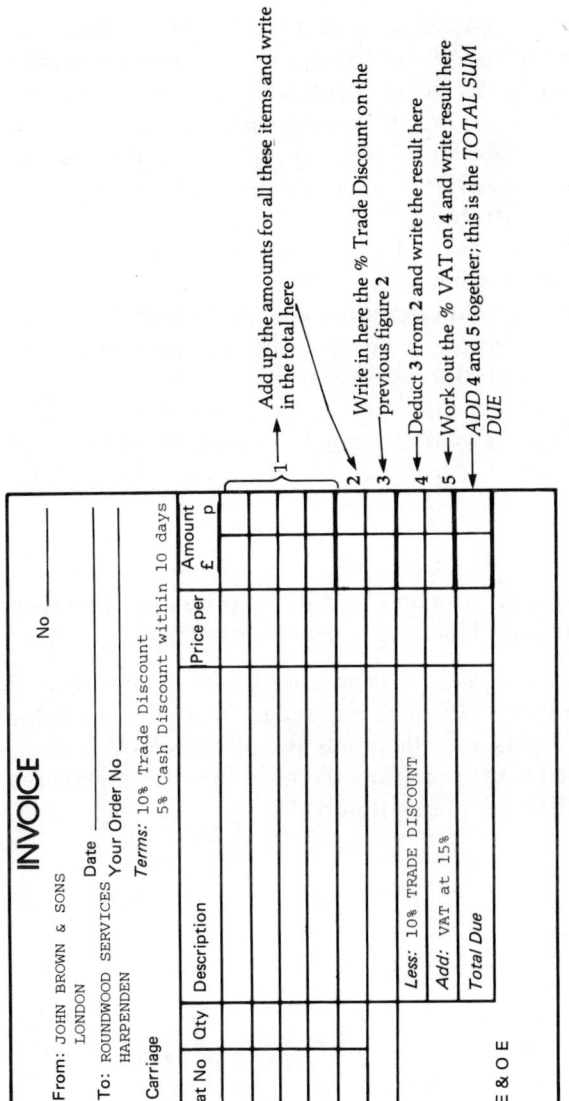

Fig 36 Invoice

Add up the amounts for all these items and write in the total here — 1

Write in here the % Trade Discount on the previous figure 2 — 2

Deduct 3 from 2 and write the result here — 3

Work out the % VAT on 4 and write result here — 4

ADD 4 and 5 together; this is the TOTAL SUM DUE — 5

INVOICE

No ———

From: JOHN BROWN & SONS
LONDON

To: ROUNDWOOD SERVICES Your Order No ———
HARPENDEN

Date ———

Carriage

Terms: 10% Trade Discount
5% Cash Discount within 10 days

Cat No	Qty	Description	Price per	Amount £	p
		Less: 10% TRADE DISCOUNT			
		Add: VAT at 15%			
		Total Due			

E & O E

Invoice (transactions) See fig 36. This is the bill for payment for goods or services rendered and is sent from the seller to the buyer, usually by post and not with the goods. It gives details of the goods or services to be paid for; names the terms and any discounts; also shows the method of delivery, and whether freight is Carriage Forward or Carriage Paid.

Note that the trade discount is taken off the total price of the goods or services *before* the VAT is added.

If the terms of the transaction include cash discount, the buyer will benefit if he pays the amount shown on the invoice within the specified time.

Several copies of the invoice are made by the supplier for use within his own firm, the most important being kept by the Accounts Department for ensuring that the debt is paid.

Italics A term used to indicate a sloping type, introduced into ordinary ('roman') type for emphasis or other distinctive purpose. *This sentence is printed in italics.*

Itinerary A plan or record of a business journey or trip. Itineraries should show the departure and arrival times of trains, flights, etc, the hotels at which bookings have been made, a list of appointments, meetings, etc, together with names and telephone numbers.

J

In the Telephone Alphabet J is for Jack

Abbreviations

JP . . . . justice of the peace

Job description/specification/profile   This is sometimes given to applicants for a position in a firm or organisation. It lists the tasks involved in the job, and identifies the position of the particular post in the overall organisation.

Details shown on a job description/specification/profile are as follows:
Job title (eg Clerical Assistant)
Grade/Salary
Department
Reporting to (superior's job title)

> An *organisation chart* may be shown here
> or may be enclosed as a separate document

Summary of principal duties/responsibilities (one or two short paragraphs)
Responsibilities (listed in full)
Additional Information about the Post
Signature of job holder
Signature of manager
Date

Jogger This machine is used to vibrate papers into alignment for stapling or binding.

Joint account (banking) A current account held jointly by two or more persons.

Justification (word processors) The process of inserting tiny spaces between letters in a word, or between words themselves, to make the last letter of each line appear at the right margin.

Justowriter This is a similar machine to the flexowriter, but automatically justifies the right-hand margin.

K

Abbreviations

K (or Kb) . . . . . kilobyte
Kg . . . . kilogram(me)
Km . . . . kilometre
Km/hr . . . . . . kilometres per hour

Key (word processors)   A switch on a keyboard labelled with a character. Pressing the key brings up the character on the screen.

Keyboard (computers)   Similar to a typewriter keyboard and used to input data into the computer and to give instructions to the computer. The keyboard of a word processor is used to enter text.

Keystroke (word processors)   Pressing a single key on a keyboard once.

Kilobyte (computers)   A unit of measurement of memory or disk storage capacity. It equals 1024 bytes or characters.

Kitemark   The British Standards Institution approval mark to indicate that goods have been made to the standards laid down by it.

L

In the Telephone Alphabet L is for Lucy

Abbreviations

lb . . . . pound (in weight)
lc . . . . lower case (small characters)
LC . . . . letter of credit
ltd . . . . limited
LV . . . . luncheon voucher

Labeller   See **Addressing machines**.

Late posting facility (Royal Mail)   Posting boxes for the receipt of first-class letters prepaid with extra postage are provided on all travelling post offices, ie mail trains to which sorting carriages are attached. Registered letters and recorded delivery packets are accepted in travelling post offices at railway stations up to five minutes before the departure times on payment (affixed in stamps) of an additional fee.

Lateral filing   In this filing method the files are placed upright and side-by-side and are suspended from frames either attached to a wall or in a cabinet.

Legal tender (methods of payment)   See also **Cash transaction**. Coins and bank notes are legal tender and bank notes can be accepted in payment of a debt up to any amount. However, the following limits apply to coins: 50p coins are legal tender up to £10.

Cupro-nickel (often called 'silver') are legal tender up to £5 only.

Bronze coins are legal tender up to 20p only.

Letter of application for a post A letter of application should create a favourable impression. It should be carefully and neatly written in ink in your best handwriting—unless the advertisement calls for a typewritten letter—and should be phrased in good, plain English, avoiding commercialisms.

The following is a guide to the form the letter should take:

1 Refer to the source of the advertisement and make a formal application for the post.

*2 Give age and education.

*3 Give details of training with details of all examinations passed, with dates, or to be taken, with the likely date of results. Successes should be detailed.

*4 Give details of previous employment, and experience relating particularly to the position sought.

*5 List any other experience or qualifications likely to be useful.

*6 Refer to testimonials enclosed, or if requested give names of referees (and addresses). *Make sure you obtain the referee's permission first.*

7 Express willingness to keep any appointment for an interview.

* If you are enclosing with your letter a curriculum vitae or an official application form which you have filled in, then items 2 to 6 above should *not* be mentioned in your letter.

but

Make sure you have given *all* the information asked for.

Send *copies* of testimonials—do not part with the originals.

(NB—*Open references* are addressed 'To whom it may concern' and a copy may be sent with your letter of application. *Personal references* are from persons who have been given as referees, and state whether the applicant for a post is suitable for the position or not. They are sent direct to the advertisers of the vacancy).

and

if you are invited to attend for interview, confirm by return of post.

Fig 37 Letter-opening machine

Letter-opening machine (incoming mail)   See fig 37. This cuts narrow strips off the tops of envelopes; the strip is so fine there is little danger of damaging the matter enclosed.

Letter-reference (business letters)   This may be the file reference of the subject of the letter, or simply the writer's initials followed by those of the typist.

Letters   A letter is a written or printed message and, apart from straightforward correspondence (including official and semi-official letters), there are many different types.

Among these are the following, to which further reference should be made: *acknowledgments, business letters, circular letters, compliment slips, form letters, formal invitations and replies to invitations,* and *memoranda.*

Library (word processors)   Also known as **dictionary**. A collection of short pieces of text, stored on disk, which is reserved for special applications, eg a disk-based spelling dictionary.

Light-pen (computers)   A tool which is sensitive to light, often used in connection with a video terminal.

Line ending (word processors)   A special character denoting the end of a short line of text, created by pressing the carriage return key.

Line graphics (word processors)   A feature of some word processors whereby boxes can be put around text, or other horizontal and vertical lines can be drawn.

Line graphs   See fig 38. These are suitable for depicting fluctuations and trends. By using distinctive lines many different statistics can be shown on the same graph.

Line printer (computers)   A printing unit connected to a computer or word processor.

Line spacing (word processors)   The number of lines in a vertical inch of paper. Usually specified as single, double, half or one-and-a-half spacing.

List processing (word processors)   A feature of most word processors which allows a list of variable information to be created and automatically included within a standard piece of text. For example, when a list of names and addresses is created, together with a reminder notice, the system automatically includes the name and address in the notice, and produces a letter for each individual.

Line graph

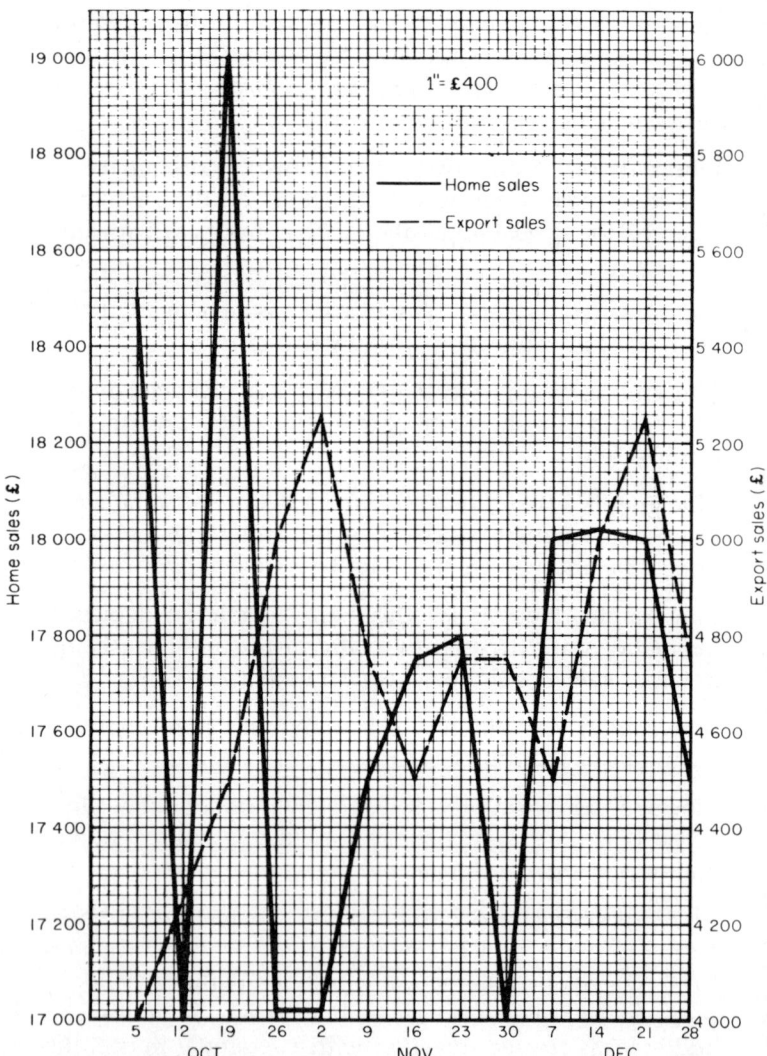

Fig 38 Line graph

Litho-inking ribbon (offset-litho duplicating)   When preparing masters on the typewriter for offset-lithography the machine must be fitted with a litho ribbon.

Loan (banking)   Loans may be negotiated with the commercial banks. Girobank will allow its customers fixed interest personal loans if certain conditions are fulfilled.

Local calls (British Telecom)   Telephone calls made from a subscriber's line to another in the same area.

Logic (computers)   That part of the central processor responsible for internal processing of the data.

Logic-seeking (word processors)   A characteristic of printers which effectively skip over any blank spaces in text, thereby achieving much faster printing speeds.

Loudspeaking telephone (British Telecom)   This equipment enables a subscriber to make and receive calls without holding the handset.

M

In the Telephone Alphabet M is for Mary

Abbreviations

M (or Mb)	megabyte
max	maximum
m/c	machine
MD	market day
Mddx	Middlesex
memo	memorandum
mfg	manufacturing
mfr	manufacturer
MICR	magnetic ink character recognition
min	minimum
misc	miscellaneous
MO	medical officer
mos	months
MP	Member of Parliament, Military Police
mph	miles per hour
MS	manuscript
MSS	manuscripts
mtg	meeting

Madam   The salutation 'Dear Madam' is used to address both single and married women.

Magnetic ink character recognition (computers)   To facilitate sorting by computer, characters (eg the numbers on a cheque) may be printed in magnetic ink.

Magnetic tapes and disks (computers)   These are rapidly superseding punched tape and cards. Magnetic tapes are coated with magnetisable material, and used for storing information. Magnetic disks are similar to the tapes, but resemble a record; they are used for storing information which is needed quickly.

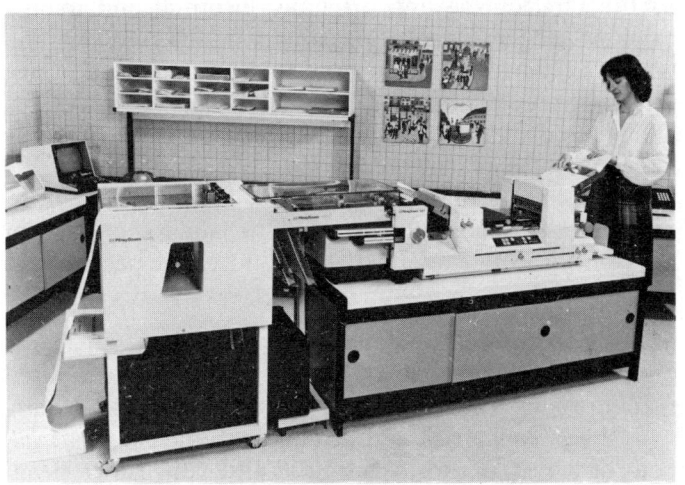

Fig 39 Mail-handling equipment

Mail-handling machines and equipment   See fig 39. In large organisations which deal with very great quantities of mail the use of automated equipment is rapidly increasing. The following is a brief outline of the machines most commonly in use; each is dealt with more fully under its own heading.

Incoming mail   A *letter-opening machine* is used to cut a narrow slip off the tops of envelopes. All letters are *date-stamped* with the day's date; sometimes a time-stamp, showing the actual time of a document's arrival, is incorporated in the date-stamp.

Mailing room/mailing department/post room

Outgoing mail Addressing machines, especially the latest *electronic addressing machines*, deal with large quantities of circulars, accounts etc. *Scales* are a necessity in a mailing room, and electronic scales can be tied in with electronic franking machines. For effectively speeding the sealing and wrapping of outgoing mail the following machines are useful: envelope-sealing machine, inserting and folding machine, jogger, package-sealing machine, rolling and wrapping machine, tucking and folding machine. Postage is usually prepaid (ie paid before the mail is sent to the Post Office). Most firms use franking machines; where very large quantities of mail are involved use can be made of the latest electronic franking machines. Some smaller firms may still use a stamp-affixing machine, and a sponge/roller moistener for moistening stamps and envelopes prior to mailing.

Mailing room/mailing department/post room In a large organisation all the mail is dealt with in a centralised mailing room, which has two distinct functions—dealing with the *incoming mail* and dealing with the *outgoing mail*, both of which are dealt with fully under their own headings.

The department also deals with mail passing inside the firm between departments; a team of messengers will do a complete circuit of the building(s) at regular intervals, collecting from departments and delivering all internal material with the outside mail during the same round. Outgoing mail is taken back to the mailing room for redistribution or despatch.

Manifolding (duplicating) Until recently the most common method of copying a document at the time of preparation was by means of carbon paper; the term 'manifolding' was applied to the making of several copies of the same matter in this way.

Manila folder (filing)   Also spelt **manilla**. This is like a large envelope and is made of manila, a type of very strong paper. It is used for plans which are too large for ordinary filing but which can be folded before being filed, and also for paper which cannot be punched.

Manual typewriter   A typewriter which is not electrically or electronically operated.

Margin (word processors)   The physical boundary of text, on the left and right side of a screen or page.

Mark (block) (word processors)   To identify a specific portion of text (by putting special codes called block markers) at the beginning and end of the piece of text.

Master copy (duplicating)   A specially prepared document which when used on the correct machine will produce a required number of copies.

Matters arising (meetings)   See fig 3. Item on the agenda of a meeting; when the minutes have been read, any business arising out of the minutes will be discussed.

Maximum stock level (stock records)   The largest amount of any one particular stock item which can be held depends on two factors: the amount of usage or demand, and the capacity of the stockroom.

Meetings (committee)   At the annual general meeting of an association, club or society a committee is elected to deal with the running of the organisation. Members of a committee attend regular meetings at which the activities of the organisation are discussed and decisions taken. The *elected officers* of such committees are normally:
The Chairman who is responsible for the proper conduct of a meeting. All speakers should 'address the chair'—ie they must get permission from the Chairman before they speak to the meeting.

The Secretary who is responsible for notifying members of the time, date and place of forthcoming meetings, and also for the preparation of an agenda after consultation with the Chairman. After the meeting the Secretary writes up the minutes which are either distributed to the committee members before the meeting or read to the members at the next meeting.

All correspondence is dealt with by the Secretary.

The Treasurer who is responsible for all financial aspects, and prepares the financial report and accounts.

Before a meeting can commence a *quorum* must be present; this is the *minimum* number of persons necessary for the transaction of business at a meeting. The number is established when the Constitution (or Standing Orders) of the association, club or society are drawn up.

Megabyte (computers) A unit of measurement of disk storage capacity, being 1 024 000 bytes or characters, ie 1000K.

Memorandum abbreviated **memo** (communications) Both memoranda and memorandums are acceptable plurals. This is a form used for internal letters, messages and reports between departments on one site, to and from branch offices, and to representatives or agents in other parts of the country and abroad. No salutation or complimentary close is used.

Memory (computers) A set of electronic components in which data is stored. Also known as the immediate access store.

Memory aids See **Follow-up systems.**

Memory typewriter This typewriter can store up to 200 000 characters (about 200 pages of A4) and instructions regarding line spacing, headings, etc. A copy of each document stored in the memory must be filed so that reference can be made to it when retyping is necessary.

Merge (word processors)   To combine units of text, or to append one document to another, to form a new document.

Message pads   See fig 40. When messages are received, either by messenger or telephone, for a member of staff

MESSAGE FOR

Mr G Clifton

WHILE YOU WERE OUT

Mr D Hobbs

Of Snows Business Forms Ltd,
Manor House Avenue, Millbrook, Southampton SO9 4WA
Telephone No 0703 777711

Telephoned		Please ring	✓
Called to see you	✓	Will call again	
Wants to see you	✓	Urgent	

Message: He would like to make an appointment

to see you to discuss a new range of

computer stationery which has been

designed to meet your needs.

Date 5 October 198–   Time 1345

Received by S Bates

Fig 40 Message form

who is temporarily absent, a note should be left for him. Message pads cover a variety of messages and are widely used. The note should be signed by the person taking the message.

Messenger   Messengers can carry business messages between firms or as an internal method of communication. Messages can be verbal, or, more usually, written. The Royal Mail Expresspost and Special Delivery Services both employ messengers to ensure very fast delivery of mail.

Methods of payment   Prompt payment in cash, or cash with order, are recognised methods of payment. Promissory notes and bills of exchange are promises to pay by a certain date and are legally binding; they are therefore regarded as fairly secure methods of payment.

The clearing banks offer current account customers the following payment facilities: banker's draft, bank giro credit, cheques, credit transfers, direct debits and standing orders. A banker's credit card is another method of payment, but is not restricted to current account holders.

Girobank also offers banker's drafts, Girobank cheques, Girobank payment services, direct debits, standing orders, and transfers to its current account customers. (Transcash is a method of paying money *into* a Girobank current account if the payer does not have such an account himself.)

The *Post Office* offers postal orders for the payment of small debts, and also an international payment service.

The Royal Mail offers a cash on delivery (COD) service.

Full details of all the above services can be found under their own headings.

Microcomputer   See fig 41. This is a small computer based on microelectronic technology.

Microfiche (microfilming)   These are single sheets of film with capacity to hold between 98 and 420 A4 documents.

Microfilming (filing) This is a way of reducing the amount of space taken up by business documents and correspondence. Documents of various sizes and thicknesses are fed

Fig 41 Microcomputer

into a *recorder* at high speed and photographed on to a spool or sheet (microfiche) of film. Provided that the documents are indexed correctly, any one of several thousand documents can be referred to easily and quickly. When reference is made to documents, the film is fitted in a *viewer*, *reader* or *projector* where they can be seen in enlarged form. If required, photocopies of the documents can be produced. See also **Micrographics**.

Micrographics (microfilming) The most up-to-date electronic filing uses a camera and a processor to store information on microfilm, in place of storing the actual documents in filing cabinets. If the equipment is linked to a computer a reader-printer will retrieve the information automatically.

Microprocessor   A term which is properly used to mean the single chip containing the central processing unit, but it can also be used to mean the complete microcomputer system. In word processing the microprocessor is a small electronic package that controls the hardware of the word processor, under the guidance of software.

Minimum stock level (stock records)   The smallest amount of any one particular stock item to which the stock can be allowed to drop, depends on the amount used and the length of time which will elapse between placing an order for fresh supplies and their delivery.

Minutes (meetings)   These record who was present at a meeting, apologies for absence from those unable to attend, and a record of what was discussed. The committee Secretary is responsible for the preparation and distribution of the minutes.

After the minutes have been read by the secretary at the next meeting (or taken as read because they were previously circulated), and have been accepted by the committee as correct, they are signed and dated by the Chairman.

Miscellaneous file   File for odd papers and correspondence for which there is no official file. If a number of papers on one matter accumulate, it is advisable to open a proper file for them to avoid overcrowding in the miscellaneous file.

Mnemonics (word processors)   Literally, a memory aid; as applied to word processing it is a code consisting of a few characters, which instructs the word processor to carry out a certain task.

Monochrome ribbon   A typewriter ribbon of one colour only.

Monospacing (word processors)   A method of printing in which each character printed takes up the same amount of space horizontally, irrespective of the size of the character. Cf **Proportional spacing**.

Motion (meetings)   A motion is a proposal put forward at a meeting. It becomes a *resolution* when it has been voted upon by the meeting and passed (or 'adopted').

Motoring handbooks   These are published annually by the AA and RAC organisations. They contain road maps, itineraries, mileage charts and details of hotels and garages, town population figures, early closing days, market days, and distances from nearest towns.

Move (block) (word processors)   To remove a block of text from one location, and reposition it at another. The block is deleted from its original location.

Multi-strike ribbon (word processors)   A type of carbon ribbon which lasts longer than an ordinary single-strike (used once only) ribbon.

Municipal undertakings   District Councils provide some services free of charge, such as refuse collection and street lighting. For many other services a small charge is made so that the cost is not borne completely by the rates. Among these are swimming pools, leisure facilities, and transport services.

N

In the Telephone Alphabet N is for Nellie

Abbreviations

NB	*nota bene* (Latin): note well
NCB	National Coal Board
NCL	National Carriers Limited
NCR	no carbon required
nem con	*nemine contradicente* (Latin): no-one contradicting/dissenting
N/F	no funds
no	number
Northants	Northamptonshire
Notts	Nottinghamshire
NP	new paragraph
nr	near

National Girobank   See **Girobank**.

National insurance   This is a statutory deduction from salaries and wages, and the money is used by the government to provide many cash benefits. These include payments to the unemployed, the sick and those permanently unable to work. Retirement and widows' pensions, together with maternity and child allowances, are funded in this way. The amount of contributions paid is related to the amount of money earned; and the money, when deducted by the employer, is entered on the Deductions

Working Sheet and is subsequently sent with the income tax that has been deducted to the income tax office.

All school-leavers are issued with their personal National Insurance Number which remains the same throughout life. It is essential that the number is retained for reference.

National Savings Bank (Post Office)   There are two kinds of National Savings Bank accounts:

1 A *Savings Bank Ordinary Account* may be opened with £1 or more at any Saving Bank post office, which will issue a bank book in which transactions are recorded. The bank book may then be used to make deposits and withdrawals at any post office transacting Savings Bank business. Repayment of deposits with interest is guaranteed by the state.

2 An *Investment Account* may be opened with £1 or more at any savings bank post office. All withdrawals are subject to one month's notice of withdrawal in writing. Payments on demand are not allowed.

Negotiable   Any document which is negotiable can be passed into the possession of another person. Such documents are called 'negotiable instruments'. Most cheques are negotiable; when they pass into the possession of another they should be endorsed (signed on the back). Bills of exchange are also negotiable. Bus and train tickets must be used by the person for whose use they were bought and are not negotiable.

Nem con (meetings)   An abbreviation of *nemine contra-dicente*—Latin for 'no-one dissenting'. When a vote is taken and no member votes against the motion—*though some members abstain from voting*—it is said to be carried *nem con*.

Net pay (salaries and wages)   The amount of pay received after all deductions—both statutory and voluntary—have been made. Also called 'take-home pay'.

Newspaper post (Royal Mail)   Only publishers or their agents are eligible to use the inland newspaper postage service which is given the same service as first-class letters. All such mail must be marked prominently 'Newspaper Post'.

Night-safe service (clearing bank current account)   This facility enables current account customers to bank moneys after closing hours. Money is put into a leather bag with a paying-in slip. The bag is locked and put into the night-safe—a small opening in the bank wall giving access to a chute leading to the bank vault. Next morning the bags are opened and the appropriate accounts credited.

No carbon required (NCR) paper   This is chemically treated paper which produces the same impression as carbon paper and makes it unnecessary to interleave sheets of carbon.

No funds (abbreviated N/F) (cheques)   Cheques marked N/F, when returned to the payee, indicate that there was no money in the drawer's account. The payee should contact the drawer.

'Nothing' comes before 'something' (alphabetical filing) This is a good general rule: a surname alone comes before a surname with an initial, and a surname with one initial comes before a surname with two initials:
Smith
Smith J
Smith J J

Notice of amended coding (P6)   This income tax form is sent by the Collector of Taxes to an employer when the tax code number of an employee has been changed.

Number unobtainable tone (telephones)   If after dialling a steady note is heard the number is out of use.

Numeric (word processors) A type of field or character that can only contain or specify a numeral.

Numerical filing One of the five main filing systems, where papers are filed in numerical order.

It is used for orders, agreements, and other documents which have serial numbers. Also organisations which have large numbers of members—such as motoring organisations and book clubs—give each member a number and correspondence with that member is filed under his number. This means that no confusion exists if there is more than one person with the same name.

Whenever numerical filing is used there must be an alphabetical card index of the names and addresses, together with the number, so that by using the cross-reference a file can be located if only the name is known. Numerical filing is capable of indefinite expansion, and though it requires a card index, the index itself often serves as a quick means of reference.

Numeric keypad (word processors) A small keyboard which only has keys with the numerals on it.

O

In the Telephone Alphabet O is for Oliver

Abbreviations

OCR	optical character recognition
O/D	overdrawn
OHMS	On Her Majesty's Service
OMR	optical mark recognition
O/S	outstanding
Oxon	Oxford, Oxfordshire
oz	ounce

Office juniors   Office juniors are employed in most departments of a firm where they will be expected to give a hand in all the less exacting jobs which are necessary to the efficient running of an organisation. Juniors are given filing to do, asked to run messages, expected to keep the office generally tidy, and will sometimes also make the tea and coffee. A junior should be courteous, friendly, pleasant and helpful, and should not feel resentful if asked to do a variety of jobs which she may consider beneath her.

Some firms will send their junior office staff round several departments as part of an induction course; the Mailing Room, Centralised Filing Department and Reprographics Department are excellent offices to work in, because there the new employee is introduced to the type of work done by a particular firm or organisation, and can begin to see the organisation pattern of the whole concern.

Officers of a committee (meetings) The three elected officers of a committee are normally:

The Chairman who is responsible for the proper conduct of meetings.

The Secretary who is responsible for notifying members of the time, date and place of meetings, for the preparation of agendas, for the writing of the minutes, and for dealing with all correspondence.

The Treasurer who is responsible for all financial aspects, and prepares the financial report and accounts.

Offices and their functions (the organisation) An office is any room where clerical work is normally carried on, whatever name it may be given.

The office is the *nucleus* of the business.

Workers in offices are employed in

1 *Industrial concerns*—extractive, manufacturing and building

2 *Commercial concerns*—advertising, banking and finance, communications, insurance, transport and warehousing, and in all types of trade both retail and wholesale, home and foreign.

3 *Service organisations*—health and education, and local authority services such as leisure and sports centres, libraries, and in Council offices.

There is an office attached to almost all kinds of business—even if it is only a desk where a self-employed person does his accounts.

All businesses need records and these are kept in offices.

The functions of the office involve writing, copying, computing, checking, filing and indexing, sorting, and all forms of communication.

Information is received, relayed, rearranged, and recorded.

Some organisations—for instance, a large insurance company—consist entirely of offices, but in many other concerns the office is *complementary* to the main purpose. For example, it would be impossible to run a factory without compiling wages, buying new materials etc—work which has to be done in an office. For a health centre to run efficiently the patient's records must be kept up-to-date and filed in order—again, this is 'office work'.

The office *controls* the factors of production by budgetary control, financial and personnel controls.

Office stock All consumable stock which is used in offices—such as paper, envelopes, paper clips etc—should be easily available when required and kept in good condition. In the stockroom the different items should be clearly labelled with their code numbers and descriptions, and the shelves should never be allowed to get untidy.

A stock record card is kept for each item, the cards usually being filed in alphabetical or code number order.

Before stock is issued to individuals or departments a requisition form is filled in and authorised by a senior member of the department requesting the stock.

When the form is received by the stock room the stock required is taken out and the necessary entries made on the stock record card. Similarly, stock being received from suppliers is entered on the card.

Official letters These are written by government departments.

Offset-lithography (duplicating) This type of duplicating can be used for any form for which there is a constant, heavy demand, and for circulars and advertisements which have a high contribution. The offset-litho machine is initially expensive to buy (or hire) and can only be justified if there is a sufficiently heavy demand.

Materials required for the preparation of masters:
The masters for offset-litho may be either a metal or a

paper plate, and can be prepared in one of the following ways:

a Typing with a typewriter *fitted with a litho ribbon*
b Writing or drawing with special inks or carbon paper
c Using photographic or electrostatic copying processes
d Using electronic scanners.

Whichever method is used the image must contain a greasy substance.

Corrections can be effected when typing offset paper plates by the use of an offset eraser made of glass fibre.

Paper required for copies Almost any type and weight of copy paper can be used and work of a very high quality can be produced.

Use of coloured inks Experienced operators can produce work in more than one colour, but a new master plate is required for each colour.

Advantages of offset-litho

1 Large quantities can be produced—50 000 copies from metal plates, 2000 copies from paper plates
2 The reproduction is very good
3 It is suitable for office forms. Large stocks need not be kept as metal plates can be stored and re-used when required.
4 It is a cheap method of reproducing large quantities.

Disadvantages of offset-litho

1 The capital outlay for machinery is high.
2 Additional office space is needed for duplicating and storage of materials.
3 Skilled operators need to be employed for the more advanced operations.
4 It is not economical for short runs.

On-line (computers) Describes a system which has terminals connected to the central computer.

Open cheque   This has no crossing and can be paid over the counter of the bank branch printed on it.

Open reference (application for a post)   This is a type of personal reference which is not sent to any particular person or firm. It is dated and addressed 'To Whom It May Concern'. A *copy* of such a testimonial may be sent to a prospective employer.

Optical character recognition (computers)   This entails marking source documents with specially shaped characters which can be recognised by the computer.

Optical mark recognition (computers)   This entails marking source documents with pencil (as in multiple-choice examination papers) which can be recognised by the computer.

Orator (British Telecom)   'Orator' is a high-quality, customer-controlled and reliable audio-teleconferencing system, engineered to suit the United Kingdom telephone network. It is specifically designed to operate over two ordinary telephone exchange lines. It can also be used on private circuits to give a discrete company network.

Order (business documents)   For the ordering of goods *order forms* are used by all businesses. They are specially printed with the firm's name and address, and the general conditions on which orders are placed often appear on them. Any instructions applying to particular orders with regard to packing, method of delivery, or route to be sent are added.

Organisation (of businesses)   The way in which any business unit is organised should be the result of planning for its own particular needs. Obviously, a manufacturing works has a very different structure from the set-up required in the head office of a large insurance company—

for instance neither a Works Manager nor a Production Department is necessary in an insurance office. The following is a list of departments which may be found in industrial and commercial concerns; a description of the function of each can be found under its own heading: Personnel, Mailing Room, Reception, Centralised Filing, Typing Pool, Reprographics, Accounts (including Salaries and Wages), Purchasing, Production, Sales, Transport. In large undertakings the Company Secretary may have his or her own department.

Organisation chart See fig 42 overleaf. An organisation chart is an attempt to portray the responsibilities (areas of activity) and relationships in an organisation or part of an organisation, such as an office. Large charts can give very little detail; more information can be obtained if a smaller area is analysed.

Orphan line (word processors) The last line of a paragraph when it appears by itself at the top of a page.

Outcard/out folder (filing) Also known as an **absent card/folder**. If a file has been borrowed from a filing system an outcard should be put in its place until its return. It should record:
1   The name or number of the file.
2   The name, department and extension number of the borrower.
3   The date it was borrowed.
An outcard should be the same size as the file it replaces, and should remain in place until the file is returned and the entry on the card cancelled.

Outgoing mail (mailing room) In a large organisation all mail is handled by a centralised mailing room, where the outgoing mail is collected from departments, and despatched.

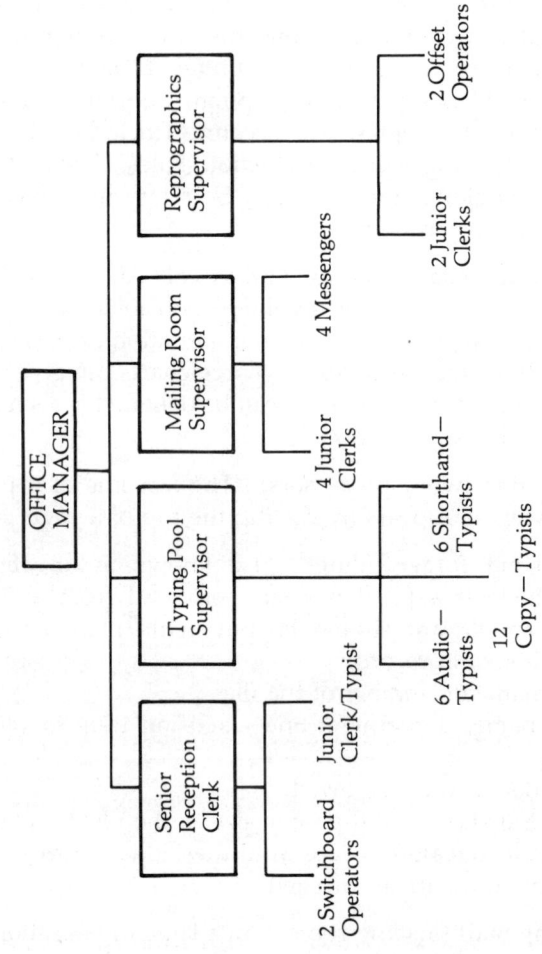

Fig 42 Organisation chart

There is usually a 'rule of the house' that all mail to be despatched that day should be ready by a certain time; at that time it is collected from, or sent down by, the different departments.

Most typed letters are sent to the mailing room with the envelopes already addressed. In the case of large quantities of routine mail use may be made of an addressing machine (qv).

Letters usually arrive in the mailing room with varying numbers of copies for routing to other internal departments. These are detached and put into the internal distribution system. Before the letters are put into the envelopes for despatch they are checked for enclosures.

In large organisations franking machines print the postage on outgoing mail, but Recorded Delivery items and Registered post should be handled separately and written up in the postage book. If any adhesive stamps are used a record of these should be kept in the stamp book (the daily stamp record).

If very large amounts of mail are to be despatched arrangements can be made for the post to be collected from the office by the Royal Mail. The service is free but the Post Office requires three hours' notice.

Mailing Rooms are making increasing use of machinery, and this is detailed under Mail-Handling Machines and Equipment.

Output (computers) The process of communicating the results of the computer's processing, often through a printer or a visual display unit.

Overdraft (current account) Permission for current account holders to overdraw on their accounts may be granted by the bank. This permits the drawing on an account of a sum in excess of one's credit at the bank, interest being charged on the day-to-day balance of the overdraft. Collateral security may be asked for by the bank.

Overtime (salaries and wages)   This covers time worked beyond the regular hours, and usually carries a rate of pay higher than the basic rate.

Time-and-a-half is the basic rate *plus* one-half of the basic rate (per hour).

Time-and-a-quarter is the basic rate *plus* one-quarter of the basic rate (per hour).

Double time (ie twice the basic rate) is sometimes paid for Sunday of Bank Holiday work.

Higher rates of pay also apply to those working unsocial hours.

Time in lieu means that in some cases 'time off' is given instead of payment. A person working on a Bank Holiday may be paid his normal rate for the day, but instead of extra payment will be given a day off with full pay at a later date.

P

In the Telephone Alphabet P is for Peter

Abbreviations

pa.	per annum, personal assistant
PABX	private automatic branch exchange
p & p	postage and packing
para.	paragraph
PAYE	pay as you earn
PBX	private branch exchange
pd	paid
pm	*post meridiem* (Latin): after noon
PMBX	private manual branch exchange
PO	Post Office, postal order
POP	post office preferred
p (pp)	page (pages)
pp ⎫ per pro ⎭	*per procurationem* (Latin): for and on behalf of
PPI	printed postage impression
PRA	pre-recorded address
PRO	Public Records Office; public relations officer
pro tem	*pro tempore* (Latin): for the time being
PS	postscript
PTO	please turn over

P6—*Notice of amended coding*　This income tax form is sent to an employer when the tax code number of an employee has been changed.

P11 (new)—*Deductions working sheet*　This income tax form is supplied for the employer to record the amount of income tax and National Insurance contributions deducted from the employee's pay. There is a separate form for each employee (see fig 31).

P13—*Emergency tax card*　This income tax form is used if an employee has no code number. When a code number is issued the record is transferred to the P11.

P14—*End of year return*　An income tax form made out in triplicate at the end of each year by employers for each employee. The top copy is sent to the Collector of Taxes for the Department of Health and Social Security; the second copy is sent to the Collector of Taxes for the Inland Revenue; *the third copy is the P60 Certificate of pay, tax deducted and National Insurance contributions*, and is given to each employee as proof that his Income Tax and NI contributions have been paid for the year shown.

P15—*Coding claim*　This will be given to an employee who has no income tax code number, possibly because he cannot get a P45 or has lost it, or because he is earning money for the first time (see fig 32).

P45—*Particulars of employee leaving*　When an employee leaves one place of employment for another he is given an income tax form P45 on which is written the total taxable pay to date and the total tax deducted to date. One copy is sent to the employer's tax office, and two are given to the employee to give to his new employer, who keeps one and sends the other to the employee's new tax office (see fig 33).

P46—*Particulars of first employment*   Form sent by the employer of a person earning money for the first time, to the Inspector of Taxes.

P60—*Certificate of pay, tax deducted and National Insurance contributions*   This is the third copy of the P14 which is made out annually by employers for each employee. It is a proof that income tax and National Insurance contributions have been paid for the year shown. This is an important document and should be carefully kept; *duplicates cannot be obtained* (see fig 34).

Package (word processors)   Name given to word processing software that is bought for use on an existing computer.

Package-sealing machine (outgoing mail)   This machine automatically seals small packets ready for mailing.

Packing and addressing of parcels (outgoing mail)   Full details of the conditions of posting are set out in the Post Office Guide. The Royal Mail also issues a leaflet 'Wrap up well', which gives detailed instructions on packing, especially that of fragile, perishable and dangerous articles, and of overseas mail.

Packing note (transactions)   A small form put into a container or package when the goods it contains are ready to be sent to a retailer or customer. It indicates the name of the person who did the final checking and/or packing and should be retained in case of complaint.
A copy of the invoice, included with the goods for delivery, is sometimes known as a *packing note* or *delivery note*.

Page (word processors)   The amount of text which a piece of paper holds; sometimes also describes the amount of text a screen can hold. Any unit of text that is separated by *page breaks*.

Page break (word processors)   A code which is inserted (either by the operator or by the system) during pagination. When the printer encounters a page break, it ejects the paper, feeds a new one in, and resumes printing. With continuous stationery it leaves a space each side of the perforation.

Page display (word processors)   Name given to a display format in which between 50 and 70 lines of text can be displayed on the screen.

Pagination (word processors)   The process of breaking up text into units that will fit on a given size of page, by inserting page breaks.

Paging/radio call system (internal method of communication)   When a call is transmitted for a certain person, only that person receives it, and the call continues until he answers a telephone and announces his availability. The service is offered by British Telecom.

Paper (stationery)   There are various types:
Airmail is a lightweight paper for letters sent by airmail.
Bank is a cheap variety of paper, sometimes called *flimsy*.
Bond is a superior-quality paper used for business and personal correspondence.
Duplicating paper The type recommended by the machine's maker should be used.
Flimsy (the same as bank) is used for carbon copies.
Semi-sorb paper is used for making copies when ink (stencil) duplicating.

Paper sizes   See top of next page.

Paper tape (computers)   Tape carrying information in the form of punched holes, used for putting information into a computer. Teleprinters also use punched tape.

PAPER SIZES

International ('A' series) mm		*Standard British* (in general superseded by international 'A' series) in	
A1	594 × 841	Foolscap	8 × 13
A2	420 × 594	Sexto	8 × 6½
A3	297 × 420	Quarto	8 × 10
A4	210 × 297	Octavo	8 × 5
A5	148 × 210	Draft	10 × 16
A6	105 × 148	Brief	13 × 16
A7	74 × 105		
A8	52 × 74		

Parcel post (Royal Mail) The maximum weight for a parcel is 25 kg and there are limitations of size according to the shape. Details can be found in the Post Office Guide. The address should be written on the parcel itself, and not merely on the label which may become detached; in case this happens, or the parcel cannot be delivered, the sender's name should be written both inside and on the cover of the parcel. On the cover it should be kept distinct from the address to which the parcel is sent, and should preferably be to the left of and at right angles to the name and address of the addressee.

'Particulars of employee leaving'—P45 When an employee leaves one place of employment for another he is given this income tax form which shows his total taxable pay to date and the total tax deducted to date. One copy is sent to the employer's tax office, and two are given to the employee to give to his new employer, who keeps one and sends the other to the employee's new tax office (see fig 33).

'Particulars of first employment'—P46   Income tax form sent by the employer of a person earning money for the first time, to the Inspector of Taxes.

Parties to a cheque   There are always three parties to a cheque: the *drawer* who is the one who signs the cheque, the *drawee* who is always the banker, and the *payee* who receives payment.

Partnership (business units)   At least two but not more than twenty people, known as partners, may share in the ownership of a firm. Solicitors and accountants can have more than twenty partners. Partners receive all the profits and are liable to meet fully any debts incurred.

Partnerships may be formed between an active partner or partners and one or more 'sleeping' partners who share the profits but can take no part in the running of the business. These are known as 'limited partnerships'; the liability of a sleeping partner is limited to the extent of the capital he contributed.

Part-page display (word processors)   Name given to a display format in which between 16 and 24 lines of text can be displayed on the screen. This is the most common display format in word processing systems.

Pay advice (salaries and wages)   Also known as **payslip**, **salary slip**, **wages slip**. This form accompanies payment of wages or salaries in cash, or is given to an employee who has his wages or salary paid into a bank or to Girobank. It gives details of money earned and of all deductions.

Gross pay is the full amount of salary or wages, including overtime pay and bonus, before any deductions have been made.

From gross pay all voluntary and statutory deductions are subtracted.

Net pay is the amount of pay received after all deductions have been made. This is also known as 'take-home pay'.

Pay as you earn (PAYE)   This is the system used in Britain to collect income tax from the employee as he earns his money. The amount due is collected from employees' earnings each pay-day and sent by employers to the tax office.

Payee   Person to whom a payment is made.

Paying-in slip (current account)   This is used by a customer paying money into his account. Books of these slips are provided by the banks with the customer's name and account number already printed on them (personalised). Deposit account customers may use a similar form for paying money into a deposit account; it is coded to distinguish it from the current account form.

Payroll (salaries and wages)   A list of all employees entitled to pay, showing the gross pay, details of all deductions, and the net pay, of each.

Payslip   See **Pay advice**.

Pay-tone (telephones)   This tone consists of high-pitched, rapid pips, and is heard by the person called when the caller is using a pay-phone (a pay-on-answer phone, eg in a callbox). Sufficient time should be allowed for the caller to put his money in the box, which allows the connection to be made.

Pending file   Used to contain the daily correspondence and routine papers awaiting action, which would otherwise be lying unprotected on the desk.

Per annum   Yearly.

Per cent   For every hundred.

Perpetual inventory (stocktaking)   This is a method of stocktaking which goes on throughout the year, and is usually incorporated in the normal running of the stock-room. It is particularly useful where the stock items are fast-moving.

Per procurationem (business letters)   Abbreviated *pp* or *per pro*. In business, authority is sometimes given to certain officials to sign on behalf of another employee. When signing 'per pro' the signature should appear *below* the name of the person taking responsibility for the letter.

Personal call (British Telecom)   This service enables the caller to ask the operator for a particular person, and no charge is made until that person is on the line. (Also known as **person-to-person call**.)
The term 'personal call' is also generally used to cover telephone calls made by one private individual to another.

Personalised cheques (current account)   Cheques on which the name and account number of the customer are printed by the bank.
Paying-in slips (bank giro credit slips) may also be personalised.

Personal letters   If a letter is of a personal nature the word 'Personal' should appear above the address on both letter and envelope. Letters so marked, when received by a firm's Mailing Room, should be passed to the addressee unopened.

Personal reference (application for a post)   This is a testimonial from a person who has been given as a referee by an applicant for a post. It is sent direct to the employer who has requested it.
Where personal references are asked for the referee's permission to use his name should be obtained in advance.

Personnel Department The Chief Personnel Officer is responsible for recruiting staff and interviewing applicants. He is responsible also for the work records of all members of the work force and for holiday arrangements. In a large firm a Training Officer will be a responsible member of the Personnel Department. He will provide induction courses for new members of staff, and technical and supervisory training in all departments and at all levels.

All employees should be regularly assessed and promotions and transfers between departments arranged where necessary. The Personnel Officer will advise on all aspects of salary structures within the firm, and may also act as a Labour Relations Officer in negotiations with union officials.

The welfare of the work force is also the responsibility of the Personnel Officer, as is the implementation of all government Acts regarding the health and safety of staff. Contracts of employment for new employees are drawn up by the Personnel Manager.

Person-to-person call This is the *personal call* service of British Telecom which enables the caller to ask the operator for a particular person, no charge being made until that person is on the line.

Petty cash book (see fig 43) This is an account of a sum of money from which small cash payments are made. A *petty cash voucher* must be prepared for every payment. The voucher will show the date, the amount and the purpose of the payment and will be signed by the person receiving the money; it will also have attached to it the 'bill' or cash ticket from a shop where small purchases have been made. It should also be signed by a senior clerk or other responsible person who has given authority to draw money from petty cash before the money is paid out. Petty cash is

PETTY CASH ACCOUNT

Dr											Cr
Received	Date 198–	Details	Fo	V No	Total paid out	Stationery	Office expenses	Travelling	Postage	VAT	
17 42	May 1	Balance b/f	CB2								
32 58	" 1	Cash received									
	" 2	Ball point pen refills		20	4 00	3 48				- 52	
	" 3	First Aid equipment		21	2 87		2 50			- 37	
	" 4	Taxi fare		22	2 00			2 00			
	" 4	Aerogrammes		23	1 44				1 44		
	" 5	Flowers for foyer		24	6 50		6 50				
	" 8	Packet of envelopes (<4)		25	1 72	1 50				- 22	
	" 12	Jar of coffee		26	0 90		0 90				
	" 15	Travelling expenses		27	1 85			1 85			
	" 21	Registered letter envelopes		28	12 35				12 35		
	" 29	Window cleaning		29	5 50		5 50				
					39 13	4 98	15 40	3 85	13 79	1 11	
	" 31	Balance c/f			10 87	£1	£2	£3	£4	£5	
50 00					50 00						
10 87	June 1	Balance b/f	CB3								
39 13	" 1	Cash received									

Fig 43 Petty cash account

usually run on the imprest system, which means that it starts off with a 'float' (imprest) and no matter what sum is spent out during a week or other set period that sum is returned to it so that the sum in the cash box is again equal to the float.

Figure 43 is a copy of a petty cash sheet. It is divided by a double line; on the left of the line are shown entries of cash brought forward (from the previous sheet) and cash received, which is the amount put into the account to bring it back to the figure of the float. On the right of the double line details of expenditure are shown, each item being entered into the Total column. To the right again of this Total column are the analysis columns, each with a heading. As an entry is made in the Total column it is repeated in the appropriate analysis column. Sometimes there is a 'sundries' column where any item which cannot be placed under a specific heading should be entered. At the end of the period the columns are totalled; the total of the analysis columns should of course equal the total payments made. At this point the cash in the cash box should be checked. When the total amount for this is added to the total payments for the period the total of the two should equal the amount of the original float (in this case it is £50). If the account is correct the petty cash is reimbursed for the period's expenditure and the amount in the cash box again equals the original float.

Petty cash voucher (see fig 44)   To obtain reimbursement for small amounts paid out on behalf of an employer a petty cash voucher must be completed, and presented with the 'bill' or cash ticket from a shop as proof of payment. The voucher must be authorised by a person in authority and, when this has been done, the Petty Cashier will pay the money out. The payee's signature is also required on the form.

All petty cash vouchers are numbered as they are entered in the petty cash book.

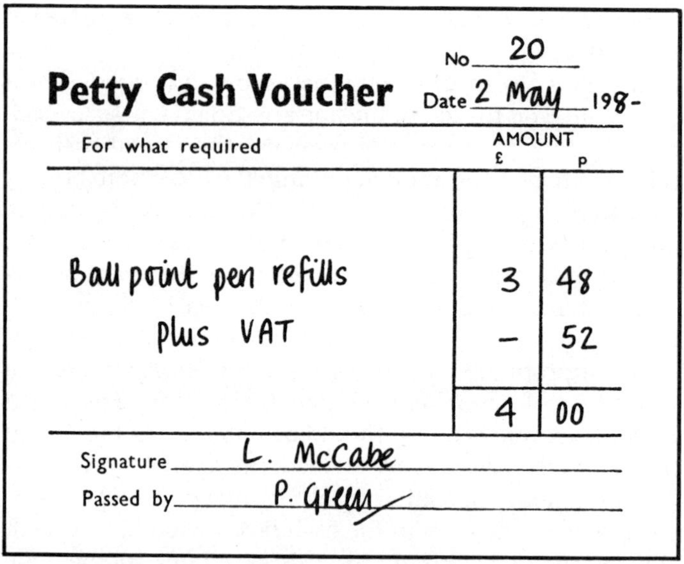

Petty Cash Voucher

No. 20

Date 2 May 198-

For what required	AMOUNT £	p
Ball point pen refills	3	48
plus VAT	–	52
	4	00

Signature L. McCabe

Passed by P. Green

Fig 44 Petty cash voucher

Phonetic alphabet This is the Telephone Alphabet which is used for clarification when 'spelling out' words over the telephone. The name or word used to identify each letter is shown as the first item under each letter in this dictionary.

Photocopiers (see fig 45) There are many varieties of photocopier; they all produce copies of an original and there is no need to prepare a master.

A *flat-bed* machine is one where the original is copied on top of the machine under a cover, and this enables books and magazines to be copied, as well as valuable documents.

A *plain paper* copier will take copies on any kind of paper. Though individual copies are expensive, it must be remembered that no labour is involved in the preparation of special masters.

Fig 45 Photocopier/collator

Masters for use with ink (stencil), spirit and offset-litho duplicating machines can be produced on certain photocopiers.
The rapid collating and stapling of copies for long reports and for booklets may be effected in one operation by some office photocopiers.

Pica A size of type giving 10 characters to the inch (25 mm).

Pictogram/pictograph (communications) (See fig 46.) A chart which uses symbols instead of figures, lines etc.

161

Piecework

TV viewing—young people

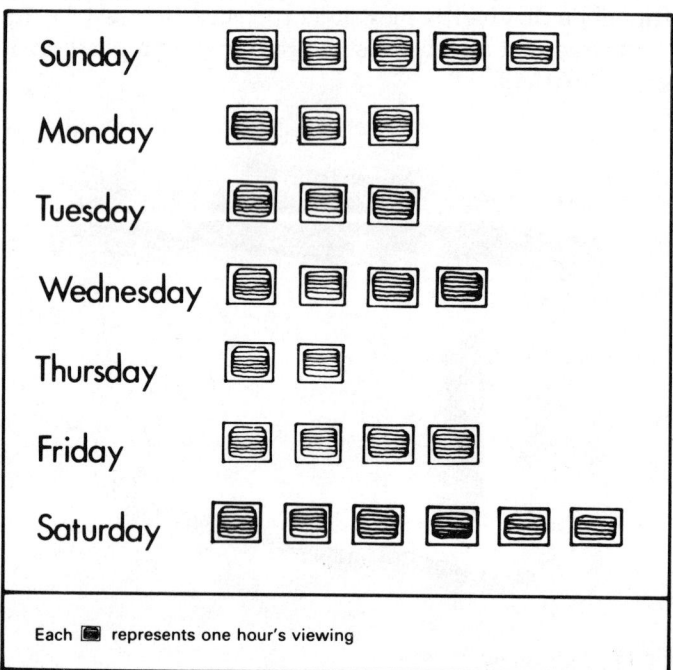

Fig 46 Pictogram/pictograph

Piecework (salaries and wages)   This is work paid for by the number of units produced, and not by the amount of hours worked. Wages are not allowed to fall below a minimum flat-rate wage.

Pie chart (communications)   (See fig 47.) A circle (representing a whole amount) showing a division into separate proportional 'slices'; used for representing statistics.

Pitch   A measure of character spacing, ie the number of characters that are printed in a horizontal inch. Also measured in characters per inch (CPI).

Plotter (computers)   A machine used for drawing plans and diagrams.

Pocket envelopes   These have the opening on the shorter side.

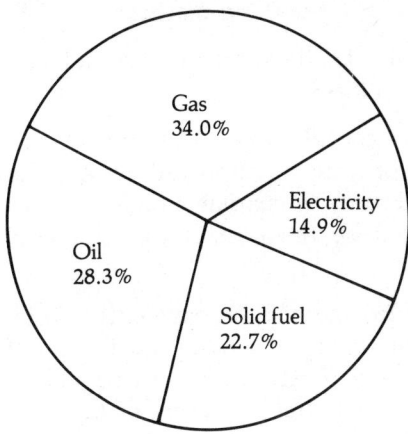

Pie chart showing British fuel consumption
(from an advertisement of British Gas)

Fig 47 Pie chart

Postage book (outgoing mail)   Most firms use franking machines for their outgoing mail, but often a postage book is used to record items which have not been franked. The postage book is usually kept on the imprest system: if the original float (imprest) is £10, then once a week the account will be reimbursed with the amount spent on postal costs and stamps in the previous week.

Postage forward parcels service (Royal Mail)   This service is designed primarily to meet the demands of business firms and advertisers who wish to obtain a parcel from a client without putting him to the expense or trouble of paying the postage. The client is sent an unstamped addressed label, wrapper or container and the parcel is posted in the ordinary way, but without a stamp; the addressee pays the charges on all parcels he receives.

Postage meter (mailing)   See **Franking machine**.

Postage rates (Royal Mail)   Leaflets on current postal rates are obtainable at all post offices.

Postage stamps (used for contributions to charity)   When affixed to books, cards, or forms of approved design, and used for collecting small sums by charitable organisations, they will be repurchased by the Post Office by special arrangement.

Postal orders (Post Office method of payment)   Postal orders provide a convenient way of sending small sums of money by post. They may be purchased and are payable at post offices, and are available up to a value of £10. The value of a postal order may be increased by affixing current British postage stamps up to the value of $4\frac{1}{2}$p; the number of stamps must not exceed two.

The payee's name must be filled in, in ink, by the sender, and the name of the post office (or town) where he lives. A counterfoil is provided on each order so that the purchaser may complete and keep it as a record. The order must be signed by the payee before payment is made.

Postal orders may be crossed like cheques; crossed postal orders must be paid into a bank account. See **Poundage**.

Postal services   Postal services in the public sector are the responsibility of the Royal Mail.

Postcheque (Girobank)   A Girobank cheque service which enables guarantee card holders to withdraw money from their Girobank account at over 80 000 post offices in 28 countries in Europe and North Africa (see fig 25).

Postcodes (Royal Mail) Postcodes represent whole addresses in simplified form. Each letter or figure focuses on progressively smaller geographical areas.

Postcodes should be used because they assist in the mechanised sorting of the mail; mail without postcodes cannot be sorted by machine and at some stage has to be rejected to be sorted by hand.

Post-dated cheques A cheque dated later than the present date; it will not be cleared until the date shown.

Poste restante (Royal Mail) Letters and parcels to be called for may be addressed to any post office except a town sub-office. The words 'To be called for' *or* 'Poste restante' should appear in the address.

Post Office Guide This is published annually by HMSO, and contains complete information on all postal regulations for inland and overseas post, the services of Girobank, Post Office monetary and investment services, licences, pensions and allowances. A card is enclosed with the Guide, which, when returned to the Head Postmaster, will ensure that amendments to the guide will be notified to the buyer.

Post Office methods of payment All Girobank services are available at post offices, as is the international payments service for making payments abroad; details are to be found in the Post Office Guide. Postal orders can be purchased at post offices and can be used for inland payments and for payments to certain countries overseas, as specified in the Post Office Guide.

Post Office monetary services National Savings Bank services are available at most post offices as are most other National Savings services.

Premium Bonds may be purchased together with other types of government securities at post offices, where details can also be obtained of the Post Office Yearly Plan Scheme. (The Post Office SAYE Scheme has been discontinued.)

Post Office Preferred sizes (POP) (envelopes)   The Post Office sorting machines are designed to take envelopes with a certain range of size. Envelopes (and cards) should be at least 90 × 140 mm, and not larger than 120 × 235 mm.

Post Room   See **Mailing room**.

Poundage (Post Office)   A small sum charged by the Post Office when postal orders are bought.

Premium Savings Bonds (Post Office)   See also '**ERNIE**'. Premium Savings Bonds are a government security. The only essential difference between them and other forms of small savings is that instead of earning interest the bonds carry, after a qualifying period, a chance of winning a tax-free prize.
Premium Bonds are £1 each, but can only be bought in multiples of £5.

Pre-recorded address (PRA)   See **Telex plus**.

Pre-sorting (filing)   If a large number of papers are to be sorted and filed, the system of pre-sorting should be used. In alphabetical filing a pre-sorter could first be used for groups of letters, eg A–E, F–J, etc; then each group broken down into single letters. Finally, the single letters should be sorted and filed away.
A similar system can be used for pre-sorting numerically filed papers. They can first be sorted in piles of 1–999, 1000–1999 etc, then broken down into hundreds and finally into an individual order.
Large *flap-sorters* can facilitate pre-sorting.

Prestel (British Telecom)   See fig 48 overleaf. This is a viewdata service and quite distinct from the teletext services Oracle and Ceefax. Teletext is broadcast over the airwaves, but viewdata signals are sent *along telephone lines from a central computer source.* Moreover, they permit a two-way service, which means that the user can 'talk' back in simple language, using the remote-control hand-set.

Prestel is the registered trademark of British Telecom's public viewdata service. The information source is much wider, and thus much more specialised and comprehensive than teletext. Because Prestel allows the user to communicate with the information source, shopping can be done from the home by using a credit card, and hotel and travel reservations can be effected easily and quickly.

Prestel subscribers are charged a rental for the use of the service, and Prestel-connected telephone usage is also charged for.

Price list (transactions)   This is a list of the articles or commodities which a firm supplies, with their prices. A price list is usually intended to remain in force for a certain time, so that it is generally used for goods which are not liable to much fluctuation in price.

Prices current (transactions)   Some commodities such as foodstuffs and raw materials are subject to very frequent price fluctuations in accordance with the state of the market. Dealers in such commodities therefore issue at regular intervals a list called a Price Current, or Prices Current, which indicates the prices prevailing at the time it is issued, the date always appearing on the document.

Printed postage impression facility (PPI) (Royal Mail) This facility may be used by customers making single postings of not less than 5000 letters, 1000 packets or 100 parcels. Customers may print or stamp 'Postage Paid' on

Printed postage impression facility (PPI)

You can also buy through PRESTEL

AIR TRAVEL
ANGLING
BEAUTY HINTS
CAR BUYING
CONSUMER ADVICE AND RIGHTS
COMMODITIES
COMPANY INFORMATION
(including Balance Sheets)
DEFENCE
ECONOMIC VARIATIONS
EDUCATION
ELECTRICAL GOODS
ENTERTAINMENT
FARMING
FINANCE
GOVT. STATISTICS
GAMES
HEALTH
HOROSCOPES
HOTELS
INSURANCE
LAW
LIBRARIES
NEWS
OIL
PACKAGE HOLIDAYS
PARLIAMENTARY
POPULATION
PUBLICATIONS
SAILING
SEA TRAVEL
STOCKS AND SHARES
TOURISM
TRAIN INFORMATION
WEATHER

Prestel and the Prestel symbol are registered
trade marks of British Telecommunications

Fig 48 Prestel services

their own envelopes, labels or wrappers and pay the postage either in cash or through a deposit account. The service is particularly useful for the mailing of circulars. PPI items may only be posted by prior arrangement with the Royal Mail.

Printer (computers)   A device which can print out the information from a computer.

Printing calculators (office machinery)   These automatically add, subtract, multiply and divide, and also list all factors and results of the calculations on a tally roll.

Private automatic branch exchange (internal telephone system)   Abbreviated PABX. A telephone system which enables extension users to dial their own external calls without going through the switchboard; extensions can also dial one another. Calls coming in from outside must be dealt with by the switchboard operator.

Private automatic exchange (internal telephone system) Abbreviated PAX. This is entirely separate from the public exchange system, but allows users to contact one another quickly.

Private bag (Royal Mail)   A private bag may be used for both the posting and receipt of mail. The bag must be locked by the owner before it is handed over, and must be conveyed by the owner only, or his agent.

Private box (Royal Mail)   A private box may be rented at the post office for the reception of postal packets which will be called for by the owner. A PO Box Number will be included within the full address of the renter.

Private limited company (business units)   Shares in a private limited company are usually owned by the family, relatives and friends of those who run the business, and it is not permitted to sell them on the stock exchange.

The word 'limited' refers to the liability of shareholders, which is limited to the amount of money they have invested in the business in the way of shares.

Private manual branch exchange (internal telephone system)   Abbreviated PMBX. An internal telephone system where all outgoing and incoming calls, and all calls made between extensions, have to go through the switchboard.

Private sector (business units)   The private enterprises which make up this part of the economy are owned by those who receive the profits from them. The following business units are to be found in the private sector: sole traders, partnerships, private and public limited companies, and holding companies.

Production Department   This department is concerned with the actual manufacturing of goods in a factory.
Its primary function is to organise the manufacturing, and to ensure that the supply of materials and labour is satisfactory; this is the major area for the *production planning engineers.*
Quality control is necessary at all stages of manufacture. Tests must be made during the work process, and the finished goods must be examined for quality.
The production of goods must be backed up by *research and development*, both to improve the products and to remain competitive. There is constant liaison between the Production and Sales Departments.

Pro-forma invoice (business documents)   This type of invoice is not sent out to show the recipient is being charged the amount shown for the goods described; it is only a description of the goods and a statement of the price. A pro-forma invoice is sent with goods 'on approval' or on a 'sale or return' basis.

Program (computers)   A set of instructions written by a programmer, designed to enable the computer to perform some specified task. Programs are the computer's 'software'.

Programmers (computers)   Those who write computer programs.

Programming (computers)   The art and science of writing computer programs (or software).

Programming language (computers)   A special 'language', such as BASIC, COBOL or PILOT, in which a program is written so that the computer can understand it.

Projector (microfilming)   When reference is made to microfilmed records they are fitted in a projector (also called a *viewer* or *reader*) which enables the documents to be seen in enlarged form.

Promissory note (method of payment)   A promise to pay a named amount on a certain date. It can be negotiated like a bill of exchange.

Prompt (word processors)   A cue or message issued by the word processor, to which the operator must react in order to have a task carried out.

Proportional spacing   This is a method of printing in which each character printed takes up only the space it needs, rather than a fixed amount of space as in *monospacing*. (Eg the letter *i* needs less space than the letter *m*.)

Protocol (word processors)   As applied to communications, it is the set of rules by which the transmission and reception of text are governed.

Public address system (internal method of communication)   By using loud-speakers messages can be relayed all over business premises simultaneously.

Public corporations (business units)   British Rail, and the electricity and gas authorities, are examples of public corporations, which come under the public sector of the economy. Each corporation is set up by an Act of Parliament, and has its own management board selected by the government, and answerable to a government minister.

Public limited company (business units)   Shares in a public limited company can be bought and sold on the stock exchange, to members of the public. Companies are controlled by a board of directors, and all shareholders have limited liability. This means that in the case of a loss they cannot be held responsible for more than their share capital.

Public sector (business units)   The public sector of the economy—that part which provides certain goods and services through central and local government authorities—may be broken down as follows:

Central government departments, such as the Department of Health and Social Security and the Department of Education and Science, are headed by ministers who are Members of Parliament, and are funded through the collection of taxes and national insurance, and other financial activities of the government.

Public Corporations administer public services such as British Rail, British Steel etc. They are controlled by a Board which is responsible to a government minister.

Local Government:

County Councils   There are 39 non-Metropolitan County Councils, 6 Metropolitan County Councils, plus the Greater London Council. The Metropolitan County Councils are heavily populated areas exemplified by the West Midlands and Greater Manchester. County Councils provide services such as education, social services and libraries;

they are funded partly from rates and partly from Government funds.

All the County Councils are subdivided into districts, served by *District Councils*. The most important function of District Councils is the provision of housing, various environmental and public health functions, maintenance of sewers, refuse collection, street-cleansing, etc. (Note that the Greater London Council is divided into *boroughs*.) To provide these local services the District Councils rely entirely on the money collected from ratepayers. For many other services the local authority makes a charge in order to cover costs; among these are swimming pools, theatres, leisure centres etc.

Punch   A small hand-operated office machine for punching holes in papers before they are filed.

Punched card operator   The basis of every punched-card system is the use of manila cards on which information is recorded by means of punch holes. The function of punched card operators is the transfer of information on to these cards.

To ensure that all the information is correct other operators work on the same kind of punching machines checking the work of the first operators; if holes have been incorrectly punched a bell will ring. These checkers are known as *verifiers*.

Punched card systems (office machinery)   Punched card systems differ from other accounting machines in that the original information, instead of being entered up directly, requires to be transferred initially to punched cards. These have holes punched in them in such a manner as to give the desired information—dates, account numbers etc. The cards are verified for accuracy on a *verifier*, sorted automatically by a *sorter*, and then fed into a machine which prints the necessary information out with speed and accuracy.

Traditionally, punched cards were produced, one for each line of information or computer program instruction. More recent equipment enables the information to be keyed on to tape or disk, both of which are easier to handle than cards, and can be read faster by the computer.

Edge-punched cards Sometimes it is necessary to select from a number of index cards all those marked with the same information. A simple method is to punch the information on to the *edges* of the cards. To pick out all the cards with the same information a rod is inserted through the cards and all the cards with the same information will be collected together.

Punched tape   Messages in code can be punched across tapes and then used in telegraphic communications, Telex and computers.

Purchasing Department   The Purchasing Manager is responsible for the buying of all raw materials and components for the production of the firm's products, and also all items such as stationery, office equipment and furniture which are required by the management and office staff in the running of the business.

Purchases requisitions for the purchase of goods are received by the Purchasing Department from all departments and stockrooms.

Q

In the Telephone Alphabet Q is for Queenie

Abbreviations

qty . . . . quantity
qv. . . . . *quod vide* (Latin): which see

Quantity discount   This discount is often given for large orders; the greater the quantity ordered the lower the unit cost.

Queue (word processors)   A method of lining up documents to be printed automatically; the operator does not have to initiate the printing of each document individually. Used in *background* (qv).

Quire (stationery)   25 sheets (formerly 24).

Quorum (meetings)   The *minimum* number of persons necessary for the transaction of business at a meeting. The number is established when the Constitution (or Standing Orders) of the association, club or society is drawn up.

Quotation (transactions)   A quotation is a special offer made by the seller to the buyer. It may be that the buyer is prepared to give a big order if the seller quotes a special price. On the other hand, the seller may be anxious to dispose of the goods, and in order to do so may be prepared to sacrifice part of his customary profit.

R

In the Telephone Alphabet R is for Robert

Abbreviations

RAC	Royal Automobile Club
RAM	random access memory
R/D.	refer to drawer
recd.	received
ref	reference
regd	registered
reqn	requisition
ROM	read only memory
RPI	Retail Price Index
RSA.	Royal Society of Arts
RSVP	Répondez s'il vous plaît (French): please reply

Radio-paging service (British Telecom)   Pagers are small radio receivers, small enough to slip into a pocket or handbag. Each one has its own number which can be called from any British Telecom telephone—free of charge. When the pager 'bleeps' the user takes whatever action has been pre-arranged: such as phoning home or the office to get his message.

Radiophone (British Telecom)   The radiophone is a piece of mobile equipment which enables the subscriber to travel freely around within a radiophone service area and still be instantly available at the end of a phone for vital talks and decisions.

Through the radiophone, calls can be connected from any telephone in the UK, and many foreign countries; with ships and oil platforms in coastal waters; with recorded information services such as motoring or weather; and with family and business.

Ragged right (word processors) Name given to text that is unjustified; ie the right-hand side of the text is not straight but ragged, and the text is only aligned vertically down the left margin.

Railway letters (Royal Mail) Under an agreement with the Post Office certain railway companies may accept first-class letters at certain of their railway stations on weekdays (and where facilities exist on Sundays) for transmission to another station, either to be called for or to be transferred to the post.

Railway parcels (Royal Mail) A railway parcel may be handed in at an express delivery post office and taken by a post office messenger to the nearest railway station for despatch by the first available train to another station, either to be called for or to be transferred to the post.

Random access memory (computers) Sometimes called the read/write memory, this is the temporary memory where data, instructions and results are stored temporarily, and where they can be referred to and altered. (Abbreviated RAM.)

Reader (microfilming) Microfilm can be viewed from a reader (or *viewer* or *projector*) and some have the facility to print out copies of documents if required.

Read only memory (computers) This is the permanent memory, the contents of which remain static. (Abbreviated ROM.)

Ream (stationery)   500 sheets (formerly 480).

Recall (word processors)   To transfer text stored on a disk to the word processor's memory, so that editing or other processing can be done to it.

Receipt (transactions)   A receipt is a business document which is given to a debtor when he pays a debt, and it is a proof of payment. Sometimes the receipt is rubber-stamped on to the invoice when the account is paid; sometimes a receipt form is given, of which the supplier keeps a copy. Receipts are not usually given when payment is by cheque.
Receipt forms should show the following information: the date; the name of the payee; the amount in figures and in words; the name of the firm receiving payment and the signature of the employee; the VAT Number of the supplier.

Reception   The main duty of the receptionist is to see that visitors to the firm are attended to promptly. At the beginning of each day the reptionist should be notified of all the appointments made and the movements of executives; sometimes an In/Out board at the reception desk will show which executives are on the premises, and this should be kept up-to-date.
The receptionist should take note of all visitors entering the office, offer help, and ask each one to sign the visitors' book or reception register. If any visitor has an appointment he should be asked to take a seat and the office where he has an appointment contacted. If he is to be sent to this office and does not know the way, some one should come for him.
The receptionist should also record all telephone messages taken at the desk and be prepared to help with typing, filing, operation of the switchboard and any other duties

which may be asked of her. It is important, however, that the reception desk should never be left unattended.

A receptionist should have a polite, friendly and helpful manner, and a capacity for speaking easily with strangers.

Reception register (callers' register/visitors' book) All visitors to a firm are asked to sign the reception register whether they have an appointment or not.

Record (word processors) A subdivision of a *file*, itself consisting of *fields*.

Recorded delivery (Royal Mail) See fig 49. This service provides a record of posting and delivery, and limited compensation cover in the event of loss or damage in the post. It is particularly useful for important documents but must not be used for money or valuables. The recorded delivery fee must be prepaid in addition to the normal postage. The address of the packet must be written on a special recorded delivery receipt form (obtainable at any post office). The gummed label at the end of the receipt form must be detached and stuck on the packet, and the form and packet must be handed to an official who will retain the packet; the receipt will be completed and handed back to the poster.

Recorder (microfilming) In microfilming the recorder is the piece of high-speed equipment which photographs documents of various sizes and thicknesses on to a spool or sheet (microfiche) of film.

Records management (word processors) A feature of some word processing systems whereby the word processor can be used to create, edit, store, sort and select, and print information that is not necessarily related to text. Maintaining lists of customers and their details is an example of this kind of information.

Redirection of mail (Royal Mail)   This is possible without additional charge if the letters are redirected not later than

This part is
attached to
the envelope

This part is
kept by the
sender as
proof of posting

Fig 49 Recorded delivery

the following day. Parcels may be redirected within the same delivery area only, without extra cost.

Reference   A *file reference* is the title shown on a file which identifies its position in the filing system. It can consist of any combination of letters or figures. Business letters often bear the file reference as a *letter reference*, which should be quoted on all correspondence dealing with the matter.

An *open reference* is a type of personal reference which is not sent to any particular person or firm. It is dated and addressed 'To Whom It May Concern'. A *copy* of such a testimonial may be sent to a prospective employer.

A *personal reference* is a testimonial from a person who has been given as a referee by an applicant for a post. It is sent direct to the employer who has requested it.

Reference books The following are recommended as useful publications to retain for reference in an office:
A good *Atlas*.

Dictionaries—
A good English dictionary
Dictionary of typewriting
Shorthand dictionary
Any foreign language dictionaries which are relevant.

Directories—
Foreign telephone directories as required—these are available from British Telecom.

Girobank Business Accounts Directory (Girobank account numbers)

Green Pages—found in some local telephone directories—contain a great deal of useful information on British Telecom services and apparatus.

Local classified directory of businesses and services with a local street map, published independently and distributed to all premises in an area. (eg Thomson's Local Directories)

Post code directories covering the UK are available free of charge to businesses and large users of the post for use in adding postcodes to their address lists.

Telephone directories for the subscriber's area are provided by the *local* telephone manager's office. London directories cover only the London postal areas, and may be obtained by application to the local manager. Note that the *prefaces* of local telephone directories contain a great deal of useful information. (See Green Pages *above*.)

A telephone dialling code directory is issued to subscribers.

A Telex directory is issued to Telex subscribers giving the Telex numbers of all subscribers.

The Yellow Pages form a classified business directory which is complementary to the local telephone directory. They list telephone subscribers in the relevant area according to trade or profession.

Forms of address can be found in *Black's Titles and Forms of address,* in *Debrett's Peerage* and *Who's Who.*

Government publications and reports can be obtained from Her Majesty's Stationery Office, 49 High Holborn, London WC1.

Hansard is the official report of proceedings in both Houses of Parliament.

Hotels and Restaurants in Great Britain is published by the Automboile Association.

Motoring Organisation Handbooks are published annually by the AA and RAC. They contain road maps, itineraries, mileage charts and details of hotels and garages, town population figures, early closing days, market days, and distances from nearest towns.

Pears Cyclopaedia is a useful handbook covering a great variety of subjects.

The Post Office Guide, published annually by HMSO, contains complete information on all postal regulations for inland and overseas post, the services of Girobank, Post Office monetary and investment services, licences, pensions and allowances. A card is enclosed with the *Guide,* which, when returned to the Head Postmaster, will ensure that all amendments to the guide will be notified to the buyer.

Ready reckoners are useful.

Roget's Thesaurus is a collection of synonyms and antonyms, classified according to the ideas they express.

Street guides are available for all towns and cities.

Timetables. All local bus and train timetables should be available. The *ABC Railway, Shipping* and *World Airways Guides* give valuable information for international travellers.

Trade journals are magazines published monthly or weekly relating to a particular trade. They are specialist publications.

The Typist's Desk Book should be available for typists.

Whitaker's Almanack is a very useful general reference book containing a vast amount of information.

Who's Who gives brief biographies of famous contemporary persons.

Year books give full details of a particular organisation or profession.

Refer to drawer (R/D) (cheques) Cheques returned to the payee by the bank may be marked R/D. In all cases the cheques should be referred back to the drawer of the cheque—he may have forgotten to date or sign the cheque in question.

Reformat (word processors) To change the format of text, by altering margins, page lengths, printing pitch, justification etc.

Registered post (Royal Mail) See fig 50. Any first-class letter or packet can be registered; it must be handed over the post office counter and a receipt for it obtained from the clerk. It must be securely sealed and money or valuables can only be mailed in one of the special envelopes sold for this purpose by the Post Office. Registration fees must be paid in addition to the first-class post, and vary according to the amount of compensation insured for. Parcels cannot be sent by registered post, but may be covered by the Compensation Fee Parcels Service (qv).

Consequential loss insurance with the inland registered post is an additional insurance offered to those registering mail.

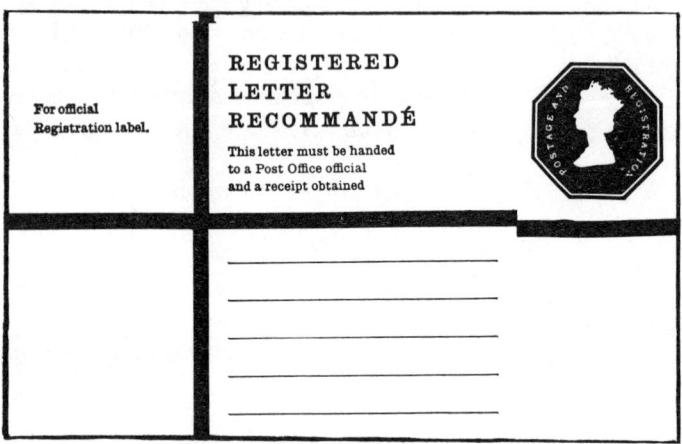

**REGISTERED
LETTER
RECOMMANDÉ**

This letter must be handed
to a Post Office official
and a receipt obtained

For official
Registration label.

Fig 50 An official registered post envelope purchased from the Post Office (*Note the cross—usually blue*)

Consequential loss is a loss to the user of the post arising out of some failure in the postal service—a loss over and above the actual value of the article lost, damaged or delayed. This insurance incurs a cost additional to the registration fee and first class postage, and is dependent on the amount of compensation cover required.

Register of callers (reception)   All visitors to a firm are asked to sign the register of callers whether they have an appointment or not. The book is also known as a **reception register/callers' register/visitors' book**.

Rehyphenation (word processors)   Inserting or deleting hyphens in text where the line length has changed as a result of changed margin settings.

Reminder procedures   See **Follow-up systems**.

Remittance   Money (in cash, by cheque, money order or postal order) which has been *sent* in payment. Money which has been passed over a counter is not a remittance.

REMITTANCES BOOK						
Date	Remitter's name	Method of payment	Account No	Amount £		Signature
198— Jan 1	Garfield G	Chq	R1162	11	00	⎫
„ 1	Palmer	Chq	T490	12	50	⎪
„ 1	Shell Garage	P.O.	R1169		65	⎪
„ 1	Cox	Chq	T499	52	00	⎬ T. Jones
„ 1	Lamb Engineering	Chq	P1119	14	48	⎪
„ 1	Sanderson	Cash	P1231	1	00	⎪
„ 1	Donald	Chq	T515	20	50	⎭

Fig 51 Remittances book

Remittance advice (transactions)   This is a printed form which is to be sent with a remittance by the debtor. It is prepared and printed by the firm or organisation which is to *receive* the money and is sent with the request for payment. The debtor will return it with a cheque, standing order mandate or direct debit mandate.

Remittances book (incoming mail)   See fig 51. This book is usually kept in the mailing room and is a record of all monies whether cash, cheques, or postal orders, which have arrived by post. All items for the day are entered and the book, together with the cash, cheques etc, is taken to the Accounts Department where the cashier signs the book to vouch for the fact that he has received the monies.

Rename (word processors)   To change the name (or other identifier) of a document stored on disk.

Re-order level (stock records)   When the balance shown on a stock record card reaches re-order level then fresh supplies are ordered from the supplier. The re-order level is a figure larger than the minimum stock level, and takes into consideration the time taken for delivery of the particular stock item.

Repagination (word processors)   The process of changing the position of *page breaks*, as may be required if text has been inserted or deleted from a document.

Replication   See **Duplicating**

Replies to business letters   When replying to business letters three points should be noted:
1   Ensure that the addressee is correctly addressed and the address written in full with the postcode.
2   If the firm or organisation to whom the communication is addressed requests that all correspondence should be addressed to the Manager, or some other official, make sure this is done and if necessary insert an *attention line* (qv).
3   Remember to quote a reference number if one has been given in the original letter. The writer of the reply should also quote his letter reference if he has one.

Reply coupon (international)   See fig 52 overleaf. It is not possible to send a stamped and addressed envelope to anyone abroad. Reply coupons may be bought at the post office which should be enclosed with the letter requiring a reply, together with an addressed envelope.
The addressee can then exchange his reply coupon at a post office for stamps of his own country of the correct denomination, which he then affixes to the envelope which has been addressed.

Reprographics   The centralised Reprographics Department of a large organisation will cover all aspects of duplicating. Spirit, ink (stencil) and offset-litho machines, photocopiers and collating machines will be housed in the department.

UNION POSTALE
UNIVERSELLE
**COUPON-RÉPONSE
INTERNATIONAL**
C 22

Ce coupon est échangeable dans tous les pays de l'Union postale universelle contre un ou plusieurs timbres-poste représentant l'affranchissement minimal d'une lettre ordinaire, expédiée à l'étranger par voie de surface.

Empreinte de contrôle du pays d'origine (date facultative)	Prix de vente (indication facultative)	Timbre du bureau qui effectue l'échange

Fig 52 International reply coupon

Required hyphen (word processors) A hyphen that occurs normally in a word (such as co-educational). A required hyphen is not removed automatically by the system during rehyphenation.

Requisition form (stock records) Form required by a stockroom before stock is issued to departments or individuals. It shows who is requesting the goods, the description, code number (if any) and quantity required. It is usually signed by a senior member of staff.

Reserve file Known also as a **transfer file**. If a folder or file becomes overcrowded it is usual to transfer the oldest material to a reserve file which is kept apart from the main filing system. A slip should be put in the current file saying where the transfer file is kept.

Resolution (meetings)   When a motion has been proposed, seconded and put to the meeting, and then passed, it becomes a resolution and will be written into the minutes as such.

Retail price index (RPI)   Every month government collects the average prices paid for such things as food, clothing, rents, mortgages, transport, drink, tobacco, coal, gas, electricity, household goods etc and compares them with the average prices paid in the previous month. If prices rise RPI will rise; if prices fall RPI falls. The RPI is periodically rebased which means that it is started afresh at a new base, usually 100. *Index-linked* savings and pensions suffer no loss when this occurs. In fact, even if RPI falls, the amount returned to the index-linked saver is never less than the total amount of the contributions he has made.

Ringing-tone (telephones)   A low-pitched 'burr-burr' which indicates that the number dialled is ringing.

Rolling and wrapping machine (outgoing mail)   This prepares newspapers, magazines and journals for posting.

Rotary file   A small revolving wheel can hold a card index system; giving, for instance, the most frequently used telephone numbers and addresses.
A large revolving system (an extension of that used in shops for postcards, etc) can house a vast amount of information. Its advantages are that such equipment enables one operator to have access to many more cards than is possible in vertical filing; less space is required for the equipment; and cards do not have to be withdrawn for reference, thereby obviating possible loss.

Routing slip Also known as a **circulation slip** When there is only one copy of a document which must be read by several people a circulation list of the names of the people concerned is attached to it, and it is then sent to the person whose name appears at the top of the list. When he has read or acted upon it he will sign against his name and pass the document on to the next person named.

Royal mail method of payment (COD) Under the *cash on delivery* service of the Royal Mail the trade charge can, on certain conditions, be collected from the addressee by the postman and remitted to the sender.

Royal mail postal services These are listed below. Details of each will be found under its own heading. (See also **Royal Mail international**)

Post services—general

a	Airmail	i	Printed postage impression facility (PPI)
b	Airway letters		
c	All-up service		
d	Certificate of posting	j	Private bags and boxes
e	First class letter post	k	Railway letters
f	Parcel post	l	Redirection of mail
g	Post forward parcels service	m	Reply coupons (international)
h	Poste restante (To be called for)	n	Second class letter post
		o	Surface mail

Express services

a Datapost
b Expresspost
c Intelpost   } See Royal Mail leaflet—
d Royal Mail special Delivery   *Royal Mail special*
e Swiftair   *delivery services*

Royal Mail International

How to send things you value through the post (See Post Office leaflet of this name)
a Compensation fee parcels service
b Recorded delivery
c Registered mail *and* Consequential loss insurance

Facilities for businesses
a Business reply service
b Freepost
c Selectapost

Royal Mail International   Royal Mail International offers many new facilities to the exporter. Among these are:
Accelerated surface post (*ASP*)   A contract service for posters of large volumes of printed paper traffic and 'Small Packet' mailings.
Bulk air mail at surface rates.
Direct agent bag service—Bags are filled with mail (weight limit 30 kg) and posted at flat rates to any address in the world.
International Datapost offers a fast, secure delivery network serving an increasing number of overseas destinations.
New contract parcel facilities—Reduced charges are allowed to customers contracting to send more than 50 parcels (or 150 kg) per week to overseas destinations.

Rule of the house   Every firm has its own 'way of doing things' and its own office procedure—such as setting out letters in a certain way. This is called the 'rule of the house' and must be obeyed by all employees at all time.

Ruler (word processors)   A line which appears below the status line showing the left and right margin and tab settings.

S

In the Telephone Alphabet S is for Sugar

Abbreviations

SAE	stamped addressed envelope
Salop	Shropshire
SAYE	save as you earn
shd	should
shl	shall
SO	standing order
std	standard
STD	Subscriber Trunk Dialling
stet	let it stand

Safe deposit facility (banking)   Banks will take care of the personal property and documents of customers; they provide locked boxes which are kept in the vaults.

Salaries and wages   These are *earnings* paid by employers to employees for specified services.
Salaries are usually quoted as a yearly figure (*per annum*). They can be paid in twelve equal parts (per calendar month), or thirteen equal parts—four-weekly—(per lunar month).
Wages are usually weekly payments, sometimes based on an hourly rate.
Salaries or wages may be paid in one of the following ways: in cash, by cheque, through credit transfer, or through the Girobank payment service.

Salary slip   See **Pay advice.**

Sales department   The Sales Manager is responsible for the marketing of the firm's products at home and overseas. Advertising and market research, and sales promotion, are part of the sales activities of an organisation. Often sales representatives (travellers) are employed, each being responsible for a geographical area.
The provision of an after-sales customer services section, handling the repair and replacement of customer products, is also under the direction of the Sales Manager.

Salutation (business letters)   Phrase beginning 'Dear . . .' at the beginning of a letter.

Save (word processors)   To transfer a document from the word processor's memory to a disk. See also **Recall**.

Save as you earn (SAYE)   Several organisations, including building societies, run SAYE schemes, and some employers will make automatic deductions from pay of the amount to be saved and will pay the savings organisation direct. Contributors may also pay by standing order or by direct payment. [Note that the National Savings index-linked SAYE scheme has been superseded by the Yearly Plan scheme (qv). Existing contracts will continue until their expiry date but no further contracts will be accepted.]

Savings account (banking)   This is similar to a *deposit account* at a bank, but is usually set up for a specific reason, eg to pay for holidays.

Scales (outgoing mail)   See fig 53. Scales showing postage rates should be available in every mailing department. Electronic scales can be linked to electronic franking machines which automatically combine the weighing, postage calculations and franking operations.

Screen (word processors) The part of the word processor that displays text, similar to a television in appearance. See also **VDU**.

Scrolling (word processors) A screen can only display a limited amount of characters. To bring the other text into

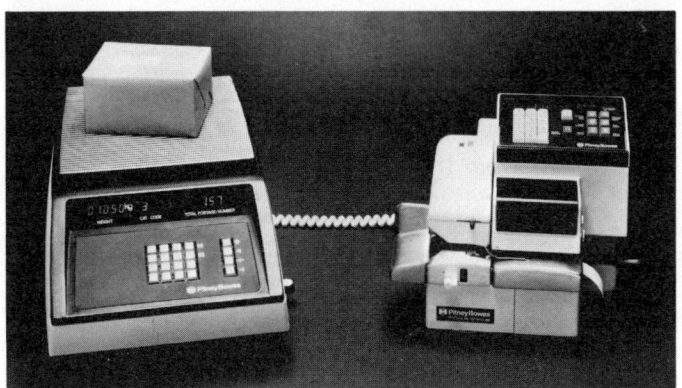

Fig 53 Electronic scale and postage meter

view, a line is removed from the top or bottom of the screen, and a new line brought in at the other end. This action is repeated continuously, giving the illusion of text moving vertically past the screen, in the manner of a scroll.

Sealing machine (outgoing mail) This machine moistens and seals the flaps of envelopes.

Search and replace (word processors) A facility on word processors by which a specified string is searched for in the text, and when found, replaced by another string.

Second class letter post (Royal Mail) This is the cheaper service for non-urgent mail. Second class letters are usually delivered up to the third working day after collection, but a high proportion is delivered by the second working day after collection.

Selectapost (Royal Mail)   This service enables a firm to arrange for the Royal Mail to subdivide the *incoming mail* into separate departments before delivering it to the firm. The service helps to speed up incoming mail in the mailing room.

Self cheque   By making an open cheque payable to 'Self' it could be used for obtaining cash over a bank counter. Now it is more usual to use a crossed cheque made out to 'Cash'.

Semi-official/semi-personal letters   These are business letters which use less formal language.
They usually start—   Dear Mr Harris
       or Dear Harris
       or Dear Ted
and end with   Yours sincerely*
       or Yours truly*
* Note the small 's' and 't'.

Semi-sorb paper (ink duplicating)   Paper used when making copies on an ink (stencil) duplicator.

Settlement discount (transactions)   This is given to debtors who pay promptly for goods when the time for payment arrives—eg '$2\frac{1}{2}$% discount for payment within one month'. Also known as **cash discount**.

Shared facilities (computers)   A general term given to either shared logic or shared resources configurations.
Shared logic   A configuration in which a number of word processors are stripped of their disks and control electronics, and instead connected to a central, high-capacity disk unit. This central unit is called a central processing unit, or CPU.
Shared resources   A configuration in which two or more word processors share a resource, such as a printer.

Shorthand-typist The efficient shorthand-typist is usually highly-qualified. She may be employed in private secretarial work, in confidential matters, and in the reporting of meetings.

When first trained, shorthand-typists often start work in a typing pool where they are sent out to different executives as required. This is excellent training for a shorthand-typist before she is allocated to one, or a group of, executives.

Shredding machines This is a document-destroying machine which shreds secret and confidential documents. Shredded paper can be used to provide packing material for parcels.

Signalling information (filing and indexing)   On all index systems information can be given by attaching coloured or distinctive signals. Similar signals can be arranged on a wall-chart so that an up-to-date position can be seen at a glance.

Simple interest Interest is reckoned as a percentage of the principal (the money invested or lent). In simple interest the principal earns the percentage rate each year, and the interest is never added to the principal to earn interest. See also **Compound interest**.

Single-sheet feed (computers)   An attachment to a printer basically consisting of a tray that holds a ream of paper. Under instructions from the printer, it feeds a single sheet at a time into the printer, without the operator having to do so.

Single-strike ribbon (computers)   A type of carbon ribbon which is only good for one pass in the printer, after which it has to be discarded. It gives a high quality print.

Software (computers)   Name given to the programs (sets of instructions) that the microprocessor can act on to control the operation of the hardware.

Soft zone (word processors)   This is the same as hot zone (qv).

Sole trader (business unit)   This is a business unit owned and run by the proprietor, who receives all the profits and is liable for all the debts. Sole traders are in the private sector of the economy.

Sort (word processors)   To arrange or order information in a specific sequence, eg alphabetically.

Sorter (office machinery)   In *punched card systems* cards on which information has been punched can be fed into a sorter which sorts and prints the required information at high speeds.

Sound synthesizer (computers)   A sound synthesizer, acting on signals from the computer, can put sounds together to make words etc.

Sources of information   The most import of these are:
Libraries which have large reference sections where books can be referred to but not borrowed.
In many areas *Citizens' Advice Bureaux* offer helpful advice. British Telecom's *talking phones* provide business, weather and motoring information.
There are also several computerised sources of information. Among these are:
Prestel—British Telecom's videophone service—for further information see entry under **Prestel**.
Oracle—the Independent Broadcasting Authority's television information service. See **Teletext**.
Ceefax—the television information service operated by the British Broadcasting Corporation. See **Teletext**.
See also **Reference books**.

Spike filing   Filing method in which the papers are put on a long spike in order of receipt. It is useful for filing the bills in restaurants as they are paid.

Spirit duplicating   The spirit duplicator uses a transfer sheet similar to carbon paper (hectograph carbon) and the coated side is placed against the glossy side of special master paper. By typing (or writing) upon the master a reverse impression of the matter to be duplicated is transferred to the back of the master. The master is then put on the drum of the duplicator and a special spirit transfers the impression (right way round) from the master to the copy paper. This method is very easy and cheap, and by using different coloured transfer sheets many colours can be reproduced *at one operation*. It is suitable however for only up to about 200 clear copies and if exposed to strong light the copies tend to fade so it is not satisfactory if permanent copies are needed. Copies are made on special spirit duplicating paper which, unlike the semi-sorb paper used for ink duplicating, is suitable for writing on in ink. It is a good method for internal memoranda and circulars.

Required for the preparation of spirit masters:

Special 'master' paper, glossy on one side.

Hectograph carbon of the required colour(s).

Correcting fluid, if required.

Required for the production of copies on a spirit duplicator:

Special copy paper (non-absorbent).

Duplicating fluid (a quick-drying spirit).

Advantages of spirit duplicating:

1   The preparation of masters and operation of the machine are easy and quick.

2   Cheap for between 20 and 200 copies.

3   Several colours can be reproduced in one operation.

4   The copy paper is of good quality and suitable for handwriting.

Disadvantages of spirit duplicating:

1   There is no standard quality of reproduction as the master deteriorates with use. After a long run the first copies are very noticeably clearer than the final copies.

2 Copies fade if exposed to light for any length of time.
3 There is a limit to the number of copies which can be reproduced from any one master—usually about 200.
4 It is not suitable for high quality work.

Sponge/roller moistener (outgoing mail) This moistens stamps and envelopes prior to mailing.

Spool (word processors) An acronym for Simultaneous Peripheral Operation On Line; the word describes how a print queue works.

Stale cheque A cheque is stale if it is more than six months old, and it may not be accepted by the bank.

Stamp-affixing machine (outgoing mail) This is used in small offices where the volume of mail does not justify the purchase or hire of a franking machine. It will guillotine, affix and count stamps, which can be purchased from the post office in reels of 500.

Stamp book (outgoing mail) Also known as the **daily stamp record**. Though most firms use franking machines instead of adhesive stamps it is usual to keep some stamps for use in emergencies etc. A record of such stamps is made in the stamp book which is usually kept on the imprest system, money for the purchase of stamps being obtained from petty cash.

Standalone (word processors) Describes a word processor which has all the components needed for word processing enclosed in one unit; ie it is self-contained and does not require any add-ons or supports.

Standard paragraph (word processors) A piece of text which can be a part of many different documents, eg a clause within a contract. It is stored on disk, and brought into the text when needed. A collection of standard paragraphs makes up a *library* or *glossary*, and is used in document assembly.

Standing order (SO) (current account method of payment) Also known as a **banker's order** or **banker's standing order**. See fig 54 overleaf. Where payment is required of regular amounts at regular intervals—hire purchase payments, insurance premiums, club or society subscriptions for instance—the customer gives the clearing bank instructions to pay these by filling in a standing order mandate. This saves the customer the trouble of writing cheques, and avoids the danger of forgetting to pay. Girobank also offers a standing order service.

Stapler (office equipment)   Small hand-operated machine used for fixing wire staples into sets of documents to bind them together.

Statement of account (transactions) See fig 55. All businesses make a practice of balancing their debtors' accounts at regular intervals, usually monthly. At the end of each month a statement of account is made up and sent to each debtor. The particulars appearing in the statement are:
1   Any balance outstanding at the beginning of the period is called the *account rendered*. This is usually an amount which has appeared on a previous statement but which has not been paid.
2   The total of each invoice for the period; the figure shown will already have trade or quantity discounts allowed, and VAT added.
3   The total of each debit note for the period.
4   The total of each credit note for the period.
5   Any payments made (usually by cheque) or discounts allowed for the period.
Items 1, 2 and 3 are debits. Item 1 will appear only in the Balance column.

Statement of account

STANDING ORDER MANDATE

To _____ Bank of Education

Address _____ 1 High Street, Hometown

	Bank	Branch Title (not address)	Code Number
Please pay	Everyman's Bank	Nowtown	00-00-01
		Beneficiary	Account Number
for the credit of	A & B Insurance Company		7 2 0 3 1 5 2 4
	Amount in figures	Amount in words	
†the sum of	£5-25	Five Pounds 25 only	

	Date and amount of 1st payment		Date and frequency
commencing	1st Sept 1981 *now —	£5-25	and thereafter every 1st Monthly
	Date and amount of last payment		
*until	1st Aug 1996	£5-25	
quoting the reference	6572		and debit my/our account accordingly

* This instruction cancels any previous order in favour of the beneficiary named above, under this reference
† If the amount of the periodic payments vary they should be incorporated in a schedule overleaf

Special instructions

Signature(s) _____ Arthur Brown _____ Date 20/8/81

Title and number of account to be debited _____ ARTHUR BROWN _____ | 1 | 0 | 4 | 7 | 6 | 3 | 7 | 5 |

*Delete if not applicable

Note: The Bank will not undertake to
   (i) make any reference to Value Added Tax or pay a stated sum "plus VAT"
   (ii) advise payer's address to beneficiary
   (iii) advise beneficiary of inability to pay
   (iv) request beneficiary's banker to advise beneficiary of receipt.

Fig 54 Standing order mandate (clearing bank)

Items 2 and 3 when entered under the Debit heading will *increase* the amount of the balance which is the amount owed by the debtor to his supplier.

Headings for a statement of account and an explanation of the entries on it

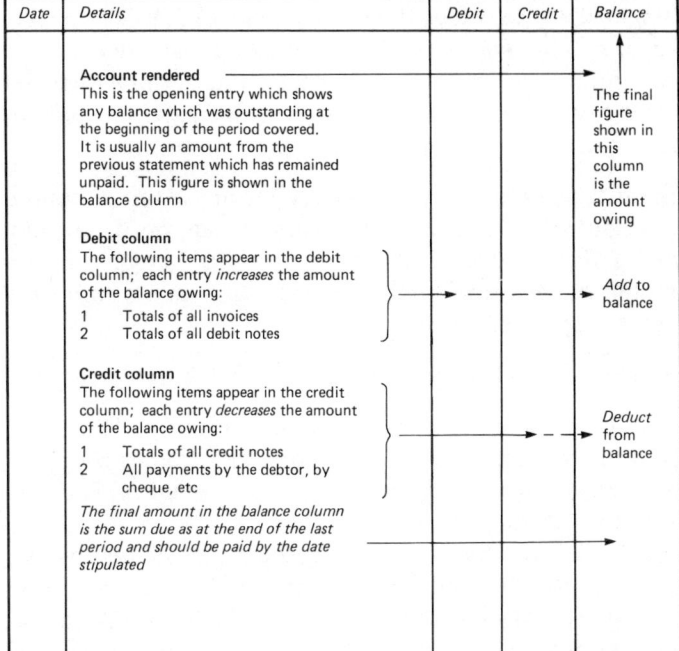

Fig 55 Statement of account

Items 4 and 5 are credits. When entered under the Credit heading they will cause a *decrease* in the balance figure.

The final figure showing in the Balance column is the figure owed by the debtor to his supplier at the end of the month shown. If the terms of transactions between the two firms include cash discount, the debtor will be granted this if he pays within the time limit specified.

201

Stationary   Not moving.

Stationery   Writing materials.

Stationery (word processors)   The paper on which text is printed is of two types: single-sheet and continuous. Single-sheet describes the ordinary single pieces of paper, such as the standard A4. Continuous stationery is a continuous strip folded into sheets, and perforated at the end of each sheet. Sprocket holes on the sides enable it to pass through a tractor feed on top of the printer.

Status line (word processors)   A line at the top or bottom of the screen that gives information about work currently being done (specifically things like the cursor position within the text, the length of a page, and any prompts the system may issue.)

Statutory   As laid down by a law enacted by Parliament.

Statutory deductions (salaries and wages)   These are compulsory deductions made from the incomes of salary- and wage-earners under the law of the land. The two statutory deductions are:

1   *Income Tax* which is a tax on incomes, levied for meeting the expenses of the Government. It is deducted from salaries or wages by the employer, at the time of payment, and is therefore known as PAYE (pay as you earn).

2   *National Insurance*. All employees make this payment, which is based on the amount of pay earned; the employer also makes his contribution and remits both at regular intervals to the Collector of Taxes who collects it on behalf of the Department of Health and Social Security.

The contributions cover many benefits including those for unemployment, sickness, maternity, industrial injuries, widows, retirement etc.

Both benefits and contributions may be 'earnings-related',

so that higher earnings earn higher weekly benefits where these are applicable.

Stencil (ink duplicating) This is a specially prepared sheet used for obtaining a large number of copies of letters or other documents. It does not really become a stencil until it has been typed or written upon, when it becomes partially perforated by the type or stylus pen. When the stencil is placed round the drum of an ink duplicating machine the ink penetrates through the stencil to the sheets of paper placed beneath, producing a copy of the prepared stencil.

Stencils can be stored and used again if desired; if this is done they should be stored in a purpose-built cabinet in which they hang downward.

Stenographer A shorthand-typist.

Stock record card (stationery stock record card) (office stock) See fig 56 overleaf. In an office it is necessary to keep records of all stationery stock used so that adequate supplies can be held and an eye kept on undue wastage. Stationery stock is regarded as consumable stock—this means it is used and needs replacement. A stock card is kept for each stock item, the cards usually being filed in alphabetical or code number order.

Before stock is issued to individuals or departments a requisition form is filled in and authorised by a senior member of the department issuing it. When the form is received by the stock room the stock required is taken out and the necessary entries made on the stock record card. Similarly stock being received from suppliers is entered on the card.

Stock cards should contain the following information:
A description of the item, including size, weight etc, and code number, if any.

Stock record card

STOCK RECORD CARD

ITEM:		MAXIMUM:		
REF No:		MINIMUM:		
SUPPLIER:		RE-ORDER LEVEL:		
Date	Req/Order/Credit No	In	Out	Bal
	Requisitions The amount			
	taken out of stock on receipt of a requisition is entered in			Deduct
	the *out* column and causes the balance in stock to			from balance
	decrease			
	Orders Supplies received are entered in the *in* column			Add
	and *increase* the balance in stock			to balance
	Credits (i e items *returned*			Add
	to the stockroom) are entered in the *in* column			to
	and *increase* the balance in stock			balance

Fig 56 Stock record card

The maximum stock level. This figure will depend on two factors: the amount of this particular item which is used, and the capacity of the stockroom.

The minimum stock level. This depends on the amount used and the length of time which will elapse between placing an order for fresh supplies and their delivery.

Re-order level. When the balance shown on a stock record card reaches re-order level then fresh supplies are ordered from the supplier. The re-order level is a figure larger than the minimum stock level, and takes into consideration the time taken for delivery of the particular stock item.

Stock record cards vary in their design. The example

shown in fig 56 has an In column and an Out column, indicating receipt of new stock and amounts taken out of stock. Entries in the In column mean that the balance in stock column will increase; entries in the Out column mean that the balance in stock figure will decrease.

Stock records   In an office it is necessary to keep records of all stationery stock held, so that adequate supplies can be sustained and an eye kept on undue wastage. Stationery stock is regarded as consumable stock—this means it is used and needs replacement.

Stocktaking (office stock)   Stockrooms should be checked for stock periodically or have an annual stocktaking at the end of each year. A physical check or count of all stock is made, and the results checked against the figures shown on the stock record cards. If the stock records have been properly kept, shortages in stock through pilferage, wastage, or deterioration may be brought to light.

An *annual inventory* (annual stock count) involves stocktaking of furniture, equipment, fixtures and fittings and is usually made in addition to the annual stocktaking of items in the stockrooms. It is needed for accounting purposes, and the information is also useful when it comes to assessing the amount of insurance cover needed by the firm against fire and theft.

A *perpetual inventory* goes on throughout the year, and allows for the process to be incorporated in the normal running of the stockroom. It is particularly useful where the stock items are fast-moving.

Stop code (word processors)   A special character used to denote the position where information is to be automatically filled in at a later stage. Also called *switch code*.

Stop payment of cheque   See fig 13. The drawer of a cheque may wish to stop payment if he learns that the cheque has been lost, or if, for some reason, he does not wish the particular payment to be made. To stop a cheque a form is filled in and presented to the bank branch of issue. Bank staff are requested to keep a careful watch for the cheque, but, as a safeguard, a record of the 'stop' is placed on the computer file of the account holder. A stop cannot be placed on a cheque issued under a cheque card.

Storage of information (computers)   This is the *backing store*, to which data or programs currently in the memory can be transferred. Examples of backing store are floppy disks, rigid disks, magnetic tapes and cassette tapes.

String (word processors)   A sequence of adjoining characters; words are strings, as are acronyms and abbreviations.

Strip index   Names, addresses and telephone numbers for each of a number of persons can be recorded on separate strips. They can be arranged in any filing order required by placing them on wall charts, desk stands, revolving units, etc.
The strips are attached to a backing sheet and can be peeled off as required. By putting the whole sheet into a typewriter it is possible to type the information onto the strips.

Stylus (ink duplicating)   A special pen which must be used for handwriting on stencils when preparing masters for stencil (ink) duplicating.

Subject filing   One of the five main filing systems. Under this system filing is in accordance with the subject matter; for instance, in a Sales Department filing may be under the type of equipment sold rather than under the name of the correspondents. The various subjects will be filed in alphabetical order.

Subject heading (business letters)   The main subject of the letter is often inserted over the body of the letter between the salutation and the first paragraph.

Subscriber trunk dialling (STD) (British Telecom)   At most exchanges subscribers can dial their own trunk calls. The dialling code for all exchanges is to be found in the booklet 'Telephone Dialling Codes' which is issued to each subscriber for use in making telephone calls *only from his own exchange.*

Subscript (word processors)   A character which is printed below the baseline; 2 is a subscript in H_2O.

Subscription (business letters)   This is usually known as the complimentary close and is the phrase beginning 'Yours . . .' at the end of a letter.

Summary   A summary resembles a précis of a piece of writing or of a report. The following procedure should be followed:
1   Before commencing a summary read through all the material and note the main points.
2   Follow the order in the primary material as closely as possible.
3   Use indirect speech (the past tense and the third person).
4   Read through after completion and ensure that the summary has been written in concise, plain English.

Sundries (petty cash)   When used as the heading in a petty cash account analysis column, this covers all items which cannot be put under any other heading.

Superscript (word processors)   A character which is printed above the baseline; 3 is a superscript in a^3.

Surface mail (Royal Mail)   This covers all mail which does not travel by air—that is, all mail which travels by land routes or sea.

Suspension filing   In most filing systems the folders are placed inside pockets which are suspended from the side rails of a light metal frame fitted into a drawer by a flat metal strip. This prevents the files sliding under each other and so prevents loss. In this method all the pockets are independent, and can be removed from the drawer with the file they contain.

Another suspension system consists of a 'concertina' of folders hanging from a frame which can be placed in a cupboard. A further example is of a 'concertina' hanging from a centre rail placed on the shelves of racks.

The main purpose of suspension filing is to keep each file in its own separate, suspended pocket.

Swiftair (Royal Mail special airmail delivery)   This is an express service for letters to Europe and for air mail letters and printed papers to countries outside Europe. Swiftair is available from any post office counter, and has special priority—in the UK Swiftair items are handled separately to give them a start over normal mail. In some countries of destination they are delivered by special messenger as part of the Swiftair service. Red Swiftair labels should be affixed to all Swiftair mail.

Switch code (word processors)   A special character used to denote the position where information is to be automatically filled in at a later stage by the system. Also called *stop code*.

Switchboard   Nearly all firms have more than one telephone. All the telephones are connected to a switchboard which is looked after by a switchboard operator. The telephones in the various offices (internal telephones) are called *extensions*.

The digital switchboard (see fig 57) has a microcomputer which provides for call queueing at busy periods, diverting unanswered calls to other extensions, the use of different

Fig 57 Switchboard

ringing tones to distinguish outside calls from internal calls, and a memory store for numbers which are used frequently.

System (computers)   An interrelated collection of objects working together as a unit for a common purpose. A word processor is a system; a terminal is *part* of a system.

Systems disk (computers)   A special disk which must be inserted into the system after switching on—it carries the software that makes the word processor work, and the operator's first task is to transfer this into memory.

T

In the Telephone Alphabet T is for Tommy

Abbreviations

th	that
TR (tr).	transfer
trs	transpose
TUC	Trades Union Congress

Tab (typewriters/word processors)   The name of a key which positions the cursor directly at a specified point on a line. (This saves repeatedly pressing the space bar.) The specified point is called a *tab setting*.

Tally roll   A roll of paper used in add/listing machines, check-out machines and some calculating machines, which records the figures as they are tapped out on to the keyboard, giving totals and sub-totals when required.

Tax tables 'A' and 'B' (income tax)   Sets of these are supplied by the Inspector of Taxes to employers for every week (or month if any employees are paid monthly). They are:

Table 'A'   The amount of *free pay* is shown under every code number for the relevant week or month. The amount of free pay is deducted from the *gross pay* to find the *amount of income which has to be taxed*.
Table 'B'   This table shows the amount of tax payable for all the amounts of taxable pay worked out from Table 'A'.

210

Income tax form no P11 (*new*)—the deductions working sheet—is made out for each employee. There are columns provided for gross (total) pay, total free pay, total taxable pay and total tax due, so that the employer is able to work out the tax each payday for each employee. (See fig 31.)

Tax year (income tax)   The tax year runs from 6 April to 5 April and is divided into 52 weeks and 12 months.

Teleconferencing (British Telecom) Audio Teleconferencing is communication by two or more groups of people at different locations. If required, it may be supplemented by video aids, such as slow-scan TV, or facsimile.
A conference between just two locations is termed a 'point-to-point teleconference'. Multipoint is the term used to describe a conference between three or more locations.

Telemessages (British Telecom)   To send a telemessage the message may be sent by Telex or telephone to a main telemessage office. It is then transmitted electronically to a Royal Mail sorting office near the destination, for delivery with the next day's post.
Telemessages are printed on A4 headed notepaper and delivered in distinctive window envelopes.
For special occasions there is a choice of attractive greetings cards designed for anniversaries, birthdays, weddings, new baby, and coming of age, as well as general greetings. There is also a condolence card for sympathy messages.
The service has been extended to introduce a multi-address facility for business users. Customers who regularly send messages to a number of addresses will have the information stored on a computer file, ready for use whenever they wish to send messages to all or part of the list. This saves time and money, as a discount is offered on 'same text' messages sent to a large number of addresses.

Telephone answering machines

Telemessages can be sent at any time up to 8 pm (9 pm for delivery to a London postal district) on Mondays to Saturdays, and up to 6 pm to all places on Sundays.

Telephone answering machines and **Answering/recording machines** (British Telecom)   These machines 'answer' the telephone when the subscriber is out or busy. The

Heading for a telephone calls record book

Date	Caller's name	Time of call	Exchange called	Duration	Cost

Fig 58 Telephone calls record book

machine makes an announcement which can be changed as often as required, advising the caller as to when and where the subscriber can be contacted.

Answering/recording machines not only answer the telephone but invite callers to leave a message. These machines can be used to take orders, the number to ring often being a Freefone number.

Telephone calls record book (use of the telephone)   See fig 58. A book should be kept by the side of every telephone and extension telephone for callers to enter all outgoing official and personal calls, whether local or trunk calls. This helps to identify telephone expenses and to assess whether usage in certain cases is justified.

If the firm allows internal telephones to be used for outgoing personal calls, then the book enables the accounts department to collect the money due for such calls.

Telephone charges (British Telecom)   Information about current telephone charges is available by ringing the Freefone number shown in the preface of the local telephone directory. Detailed information leaflets are available.

For the purpose of calculating charges for calls between places within the United Kingdom, telephone exchanges are arranged in telephone groups. A call made to an exchange within the same group or to an exchange in an adjacent group is generally a local call. Other calls are generally charged on the basis of the distance between the charging point in the group in which the call originates and that in the group containing the called exchange; the 3 categories of trunk call are:

1   Calls up to 56 km (35 miles) excluding local calls.

2   Calls over 56 km (35 miles).

3   Calls over 56 km (35 miles) connected over 'low cost routes'. These are routes which carry a large number of calls, and lower charges will apply for calls connected over these routes.

The charges for these calls are based on the time allowed per charge unit on any one call. Calls connected by the *operator* are charged for the first three minutes, and thereafter for each additional minute.

Charges for telephone calls also depend upon the time of day during which they are made. These are as follows:

8.00 am–9.00 am	standard rate
9.00 am–1.00 pm	peak rate
1.00 pm–6.00 pm	standard rate
6.00 pm–8.00 pm	cheap rate

Cheap rates also apply to Bank Holidays, weekends etc.

Charges for *international calls* are at the Cheap rate from

213

Monday to Friday 8 pm to 8 am, and all weekend (UK time), where available. The Standard rates apply at all other times.

Telephone credit card (British Telecom)   The cardholder is able, by quoting his card number to the operator, to make a call from any telephone at any time, on credit. These calls are charged to the subscriber's account, an additional charge being made.

Telephone directories   These are supplied by British Telecom's local office for the subscriber's area. London directories covering the London postal areas, and directories for other areas, may be obtained by application to the local manager. Note that the *prefaces* of local telephone directories contain a great deal of useful information.

A telephone dialling code directory is issued to subscribers; each booklet gives the codes applicable to that particular exchange's local use.

Telephone message pad   Beside every office telephone there should be a message pad, so that if a message is received for a member of staff who is temporarily absent, a message can be left for him or her. The note should be signed by the person taking the message. (See fig 40.)

Telephone messages taken by British Telecom   Telephone subscribers can now ask British Telecom to answer their incoming calls if the subscriber is absent from his home or office. There are two kinds of message service:

Returned message service. The operator will answer the calls and offer to take a brief message (usually not exceeding 20 words). These messages are available to the subscriber at any time simply by calling a specially allocated number in the telephone exchange.

Whereabouts message service. The operator will answer the calls and pass on any messages the subscriber has left concerning his whereabouts.

Telephone systems (communications)   These are used for internal communications by telephone, and also for contacting other firms and organisations. For details of PAX (Private Automatic Exchange), PABX (private automatic branch exchange), and PMBX (private manual branch exchange) see **Internal telephone systems**.

Nearly all firms have more than one telephone, and all telephones may be connected to a switchboard. The telephones in the various offices are then called extensions.

Telephone, use of the   A great deal of business is transacted over the telephone and it is essential for all employees to be able to use the telephone efficiently and to convey a favourable impression of the firm or organisation when speaking to someone outside.

The telephone should always be answered promptly, and once the call is answered it is most important that the caller is not kept waiting unnecessarily as telephone calls are costly. The following suggestions may be useful:

1   Announce the name of the firm or the extension number and department. Do not say 'Hello'.

2   If the person required by the caller is not available a message should be left for him or her if the caller wishes to be contacted. A message pad and pencil should be left by each telephone for this purpose. (See fig 40.)

3   Be courteous at all times, but as brief as possible.

4   Speak slowly and distinctly; try to pitch the voice lower than the normal speaking voice—high-pitched speech does not transmit well.

5   All office workers should be familiar with the following telephone tones: dialling tone, engaged tone, number-unobtainable tone, pay tone, and ringing tone.

6   All office workers should be aware of the extent of their own local telephone area—this is shown on a map at the front of local telephone directories—and be able to make

trunk (STD) and international (now mostly IDD) calls by reference to the Dialling Codes Directory.

7   Everyone should be conversant with the telephone charges for the different times of day, and should know when the cheaper rates prevail.

8   An index of frequently-used telephone numbers should be easily accessible. In this respect a Callmaker is a useful piece of equipment; it stores frequently-used telephone numbers and enables the subscriber to save time by automatic dialling of these numbers.

9   A telephone calls record book should be kept by the side of every telephone for callers to enter all outgoing official and personal calls. This helps to identify telephone expenses and to assess whether usage in certain cases is justified.

Telephone writer   This equipment transmits handwritten messages and sketches to any number of receiving stations and can be connected to a telephone.

Telephonist   If a firm is equipped with a PMBX (Private manual branch exchange) the telephone operator deals with all incoming calls from outside the firm, and then connects the caller to the extension asked for. The same operator can connect the internal telephones of the firm, numbers being asked for by the extension callers.

If the firm has a PABX (private automatic branch exchange) incoming calls are dealt with by the switchboard operator, but internal calls between extensions can be dialled automatically without going through the switchboard.

The PABX also has facilities for allowing extension callers to dial outside calls.

The telephonist in a large organisation often has a microphone on which broadcasts can be made on a loudspeaker system (Tannoy) to all parts of the works or office complex. The control of a radio-paging system is usually situated in the same room as the switchboard, and is operated by one of the telephonists.

Teleprinters (Office machinery)   This is a telegraph transmitter with a typewriter keyboard. Most teleprinters are part of the Telex system operated by British Telecom, but they can also be used within an organisation to enable printed messages to pass between sections through an internally wired circuit; lines may be rented from British Telecom by firms and organisations.

Teleprinters offer three distinct advantages to their users:

1   It is as quick as making a telephone call, but both sender and receiver have a printed message.

2   Messages can be received out of office hours as the messages are recorded automatically.

3   It is particularly useful for international use as the time difference does not matter—messages are delivered equally effectively at any time of day or night.

Teletex (British Telecom)   The British Telecom Teletex service offers a new method of electronic communication, enabling businesses to transmit, receive and reproduce typed letters or messages using special communicating typewriter terminals. An A4 page of text can be sent in less than 10 seconds.

With its fast transmission and ease of operation it will provide significant advantages over the Telex system.

Teletext (sources of information)   Teletext is a service broadcast by the BBC and ITV which provides all kinds of up-to-the-minute information and entertainment on the television screen. It is just like a televised news magazine updated hourly by a team of sub-editors making available about 1000 pages of general sports, financial and other news, plus a whole range of entertaining topics.

The BBC have separate Teletext services called CEEFAX on

BBC1 and BBC2, while ITV call their Teletext service ORACLE.

Do not confuse with Teletex (qv).

Telex (British Telecom) This is the teleprinter service offered by British Telecom. It is a 24-hour service for the rapid interchange of printed messages between subscribers in this country and for communication with subscribers in many countries overseas, including the USA.

Subscribers rent from Telecom a teleprinter and a line to the nearest Telex exchange. In appearance the teleprinter resembles an ordinary typewriter with a telephone dial attachment.

Calls are made by direct subscriber dialling to all UK subscribers and to most European countries. When the connection has been made to the other subscriber the caller types his message, which is printed simultaneously on *both* machines. Each copy contains printed confirmation that the connection has been made (*call-back code*) and that the messages and replies from the other subscriber have been correctly received. These printed messages constitute a permanent record of the information that has been exchanged and can be filed in both offices.

Telex messages may be sent to a subscriber even when his teleprinter is unattended (eg at night); the message will then be available when the office opens.

The Telex numbers of Telex subscribers are listed in a *Telex directory*.

Those who are not Telex subscribers can have telegrams sent by British Telecom to Telex subscribers. The same service will also deliver to non-subscribers messages sent by Telex subscribers.

Telex messages can be prepared beforehand using paper tape or a special Telex cutter; this is cheaper and saves time. See also **Telex Plus**.

Telex directory (British Telecom) This is issued to all Telex subscribers and gives the numbers of all other subscribers. It also contains information about the Telex services available.

Telex Plus (British Telecom) Busy international Telex lines mean that a Telex operator can spend all day trying to get a message through. By the use of micro-processors which have memories, Telex Plus offers a facility which enables Telex messages to be sent to anyone in the United Kingdom or abroad without the subscriber having to make the contact himself. All the operator has to do is send the message via the Telex Plus computer which will then store and forward it as soon as the lines are free.

The *same* Telex message can be automatically transmitted to as many as a hundred destinations. This service is called the *Telex Plus pre-recorded address service* and is abbreviated PRA.

By tapping in the PRA codes the same message will be delivered to all the firm's addressees on the list, or to selected addresses on the list.

Temporary transfer of calls (British Telecom) This service allows for calls to be transferred from one number to another for definite periods of time.

Tender (business documents) A tender, like an estimate, is an offer to undertake specified work at a given price. It is often used in connection with contracts placed annually by local authorities for the supply of uniforms, stationery, and other necessary supplies. Very large home or overseas contracts such as the building of hospitals, dams, roads, etc are advertised in the press and tenders invited.

Terminal (computers) A machine used for sending in-formation to a computer and receiving information from a computer. It often consists of a keyboard and/or visual display unit that is connected to a computer and can be used for the remote entry and receipt of information.

Text (word processors) Letters, numbers, words and other symbols that make up a body of information. Pictures are generally excluded from text.

Text editor/text processor These are alternative names for a **word processor**.

Text register (word processors) A special temporary storage place for *blocks* that are being copied.

Time and a half (salaries and wages) This is the basic rate of pay per hour *plus* one half of the basic rate, and covers certain times worked beyond the normal hours.

Time and a quarter (salaries and wages) This is the basic rate of pay per hour *plus* one quarter of the basic rate, and covers certain times worked beyond the normal hours.

Time-card/clockcard (salaries and wages) If the 'clocking on' system is used each worker is given a time-card which he inserts into the time-recording machine on arrival at and departure from his place of work. This records automatically the correct time, which appears on the card. The cards are kept in racks by the side of the clock, and are used in assessing overtime, lateness, etc.
If the cards are numbered the number is referred to as the 'clock number', and is often used as the reference number of that particular worker by the Personnel Department.

Time in lieu (salaries and wages) This means that in some cases 'time off' is given instead of payment. A person working on a Bank Holiday may be paid his normal rate for the day, and instead of extra payment will be given a day off with full pay at a later date.

Timetables (reference books) All local bus and train

timetables should be available in an office, as well as the *ABC Railway, Shipping* and *World Airways Guides* which give valuable information for international travellers.

Tractor feed (computers)   An attachment to a printer that feeds continuous stationery through, using two circular belts with protruding studs that catch the sprocket holes in the stationery.

Trade discount (transactions)   This describes the discount given by one trader to another trader, and also the reduction in the catalogue price of an article, given by the wholesaler or manufacturer to the retailer to enable him to make a profit.

Transactions   The word 'transaction' implies a transfer of goods or services from one person to another. Where the transaction involves immediate payment for goods or services it is a *cash transaction*. Where payment is delayed until a later date it is a *credit transaction*.

Transactions are usually initiated by the sending of an *enquiry*, or (as in the case of a large contract) by the inviting of *tenders*.

An *enquiry* can be sent on a special *enquiry form* if it is for routine supplies, but sometimes it is sent in the form of a business letter. Several likely suppliers are usually circulated by the would-be buyer.

Tenders are usually 'invited' by advertisement in the press, so that any firm interested in procuring the contract can submit its tender to the advertiser.

When enquiries have been received or tenders invited the prospective suppliers send to the possible purchaser:

An *estimate* which is an estimated cost for particular goods or services and must be worked out for each enquirer

or

A *quotation* which is the price charged by a particular supplier. *Quotations* are often accompanied by *price-lists* or *catalogues*; sometimes they are given as *firm offers* which are only available if the order is received by a certain date.

or

Tenders are submitted by competing firms who are endeavouring to obtain a particular order or contract. They have usually been invited by large public bodies or local authorities and can involve the building of a dam, hospital or school at home or overseas, tree-felling for a local authority, etc.

When the purchaser decides who is to supply the required goods or services he sends an *order* to the chosen supplier.

When the goods are ready for despatch an *advice* or *despatch note* is sent to tell the customer that his order has been sent from the warehouse or factory, and the method by which it will be delivered.

With the goods when they arrive there should be a *packing* or *delivery note* stating what is being delivered at that particular time. It should be checked to see there are no discrepancies. Often the *delivery note* is signed by the customer and returned to the vanman. Sometimes there is a copy for the customer to retain which also acts as an invoice or bill.

A *consignment note* covers all the goods delivered at any one time—whether all or part of an order.

After delivery the invoice or bill is sent. For occasional transactions with a firm this should be regarded as the bill for payment. If there are many and frequent transactions with the same firm, monthly *statements of account*, showing exactly what has happened to the customer's account in the course of a month, are sent.

Sometimes a *pro forma invoice* is sent, but this should not be regarded as a bill to be paid like an ordinary invoice. It is sometimes sent with goods 'on approval'.

Credit notes are sent to credit a debtor with a certain amount and reduce the amount of an invoice.

Debit notes are an extra charge to the invoice and increase the amount the debtor owes the supplier.

Statements of account are sent out to account customers each month and give a record of all payments to the supplier and debts incurred by him during the month. If the debtor has failed to pay the previous account, or has only partially paid it, the debt is brought forward to the new account and is shown as an *account rendered*. The final figure on the statement of account is the amount owed by the buyer on the last day of the previous month.

The cost of goods and services can be reduced by *discounts*. If settlement of a debt is made in cash a *receipt* is usually given. Receipts for other methods of payment will be given if asked for.

Transcash (Girobank)   See fig 27. Cash payments can be made at post offices to people and organisations with Girobank accounts *by persons without Girobank accounts*. Transcash forms are available at post offices and many organisations also incorporate them in their bills. Transcash is convenient for the payment of bills as it avoids the cost of envelopes and postage, though a fee is charged.

A message to the payee may be written on the back of a Transcash form but the Post Office will not accept responsibility for the authenticity of any message or for any unauthorised alteration of it. *Transcash freepay* is used when the payee organisation pays the transaction fee.

Transfer file   If a folder or file becomes overcrowded it is usual to transfer the oldest material to a *reserve file* which is kept apart from the main filing system. A slip should be put in the current file saying where the transfer file is kept.

Transfer/deposit forms (Girobank)   See figs 28/29. These are used by Girobank current account customers for:
1   Paying *cash* into their own account at a Post Office.

223

2   Paying *cheques* into their own account. Cheques may not be deposited at a Post Office but must be sent direct to National Girobank at Bootle, with a completed transfer/deposit form.

3   For transferring money from one Girobank account to another Girobank account.

The *international transfer form* is used for making payments overseas.

Transferred charge calls (British Telecom)   Telephone charges may be *reversed*; this means that the person *receiving* the call pays for it, if the receiver agrees to accept it. A small fee is charged.

Transfer sheet (spirit duplicating)   This is *hectograph carbon* which is used in the preparation of a spirit master; the coated side is placed against the glossy side of special master paper. By typing (or writing) upon the master a reverse impression of the matter to be duplicated is transferred to the back of the master.

Transport department   The Chief Transport Officer is responsible for the safe despatch of all products produced by the firm. Unless the company is small it will have its own 'fleet' of vehicles, and the Transport Department is responsible for the administration involved in the fleet's running schedules and maintenance.

Planning of deliveries is necessary so that vehicles will be routed to provide maximum coverage of delivery points with a minimum vehicle mileage.

Trap packets (stationery)   These are envelopes having an opening large enough to entrap small letters and postcards. If large, unsealed envelopes are used the Royal Mail demands that senders should use envelopes with a special kind of flap (anti-trap envelopes) which can be adjusted so as not to leave a large opening.

Traveller's cheque (banking and Girobank) The traveller's cheque provides a safe and convenient way of carrying money. Traveller's cheques may be cashed not only at the branches of all the main banks in the British Isles, but also in most banks abroad, and they are frequently accepted at hotels and by large shops. They may be purchased in British or foreign currencies.

Thomas Cook traveller's cheques and foreign currency may be ordered at most post offices by Girobank customers.

Triplicate In sets of three.

Trunk calls (British Telecom) Telephone calls made to subscribers outside the subscriber's local area. If there is no STD code for the exchange being called connection is made through the operator. A booklet—*Telephone Dialling Codes*—is issued to every subscriber; it lists the codes to be used from his *local* exchange.

Tucking and folding machine (outgoing mail) These prepare notices which are to be mailed without covers.

Typeface Also known as **typestyle** or **font**, it is a set of characters of a particular style and size.

Typesetting machine (office machinery) When duplicating on this printing machine the 'master' from which the copies are made consists of metal type set up on a circular drum. The machine is capable of running off an unlimited number of copies at the rate of approximately 6000 an hour.

Typewriter ribbons These are available in one colour (monochrome) or two colours—usually black/red (bichrome). *Carbon ribbons* give a high quality finish to typewritten work but can only be used once. For preparing masters for offset-lithography a *litho-inking* ribbon should be used.

Typewriters   Most typewriters manufactured today are electric or electronic, though there are still many manual typewriters in use.

Electronic typewriters and word processors are dealt with fully under their own headings.

Typing pool   A typing pool where all typing services are concentrated in one room is an alternative to the allocation of typists to different departments; it has two main advantages. First, under the supervision of an efficient manager, the work can be more evenly distributed, and an overall method of presentation and display maintained; also the absence through illness of one typist can be less burdensome when it does not affect a particular department, but is 'spread' over all sections of the firm.

The second advantage is that the typing pool can provide an excellent training centre where junior typists can be trained initially on routine work.

Copy-typists, audio-typists and *shorthand-typists* can all be employed in the same typing pool.

Typing pools are generally unpopular and there is a tendency nowadays to allocate several typists to work as a small 'pool' to cover one department. The typists become specialists in one field, which adds to the general efficiency. At the same time the secretarial posts involving one shorthand-typist being allocated to one executive are becoming less common.

U

In the Telephone Alphabet U is for Uncle

Abbreviations

uc.	upper case (capital letters)
UK	United Kingdom
USA	United States of America
USSR	Union of Soviet Socialist Republics

Unbundled (word processors) Describes a system in which the components are given separate prices; the system is built by selecting the required components, and the total price is then calculated.

Underlining (word processors) A feature of word processors in which text is automatically underlined as it is entered.

Union dues These are membership fees which trade unionists pay to their particular union. In some organisations the dues are deducted from pay and the total collected remitted to the union. In such cases the dues are classed as a *voluntary deduction* from a salary or wage.

Unjustified (word processors) The name given to text that has not been *justified*; the right-hand side of the text is ragged and hence called *ragged right*.

Update (computers) To amend stored information to bring it up to date.

V

In the Telephone Alphabet V is for Victory

Abbreviations

VAT	value added tax
VDU	visual display unit
via	by way of
VIP	very important person
viz	*videlicet* (Latin): namely; that is to say
VN	voucher number

Value added tax (VAT) (transactions)   This is a tax levied by the Government on goods and services in business transactions; it is therefore a commercial tax. A standard rate of tax is payable on any goods and services which fall within the scope of the tax; it is collected by HM Customs and Excise.

Zero-rated goods and services carry no value added tax.

Whenever a trader buys goods or services to which VAT applies, he receives from the supplier a tax invoice indicating the cost of the goods and the tax charged on them. When, in turn, the trader supplies taxable goods and services to his customers he charges them tax at the same rate. At regular intervals, normally every quarter, the trader makes a tax return to Customs and Excise, showing the tax charged to him (*input tax*) and the tax he has charged his customers (*output tax*) and will pay the difference.

Tax point is the time when VAT becomes chargeable and is usually the date when goods or services are delivered or invoiced.

Variable (word processors)   A piece of information that varies from document to document, such as a name in a circular letter. Variables are stored as a list on disk.

Varityper (office machinery)   This is an electrically operated variable typewriter; the typist is provided with a variety of changeable styles and sizes of type, as well as the means of obtaining a perfectly even right-hand margin (automatic 'justification'), thus enabling him or her to produce typewritten work that closely resembles print. The use of a carbon ribbon further enhances clarity of impression.

Verbatim   Word for word; eg Hansard is a full record (verbatim report) of each day's proceedings in both Houses of Parliament.

Verifier (office machinery)   The basis of every punched-card system is the use of manila cards on which information is recorded by means of punch holes. To ensure that all the information punched on to the cards is correct, a second set of operators work on the same kind of punching machines checking the work of the first operators; these checkers are known as verifiers.

Vertical filing   In this filing method flat files or manila folders are placed vertically and side-by-side in the drawers of a cabinet.

Video terminal (computers)   A computer terminal with a 'television' screen.

Viewdata   Viewdata signals are sent along telephone lines from a central computer source to appear on a television screen. The service offered is two-way—the user can 'talk' back in simple language, using the remote control handset.

Prestel is the registered trademark of British Telecom's public viewdata service. (See fig 48.)

Viewer (microfilming)   When reference is made to micro-filmed records they are fitted in a viewer (also called a **projector** or **reader**) which enables the documents to be seen in enlarged form.

Visible-edge card index system   A system in which information is immediately visible without moving the cards. These can be held flat in metal drawers which fit into a cabinet, or filed on a revolving wheel. Cards are housed in such a way that they overlap each other, and the title of each is clearly visible. Colour markers (signals) or indicators may be affixed to the cards to focus attention on vital facts.

Visiting card (reception)   A visitor from another firm may offer the receptionist a business visiting card, showing his name, firm, and position in the firm.

Visitors' book **(callers' register/reception register)**   All visitors to a firm are asked to sign the visitors' book whether they have an appointment or not.

Visual display unit (VDU) (computers)   Similar to a tele-vision screen, this can display text or diagrams as output from a computer.

Voice synthesizer (computers)   A device for creating voice-like sounds from computer data.

Voluntary deductions from salaries and wages   The following is a list of possible 'voluntary' deductions, as opposed to 'statutory deductions' (qv) such as income tax and National Insurance.

1   *Private medical insurance* (BUPA, etc).
2   *SAYE (save as you earn)*   Several organisations, including building societies, run SAYE schemes; contributors may pay by standing order or by direct payment. The National Savings index-linked scheme has been superseded by the *yearly plan scheme* (qv).
3   *Social clubs and welfare schemes.* Most large firms run these and each employee is expected to contribute a set weekly or monthly figure towards the running of them. The amount is deducted from salary or wages before the employee is paid.
4   *Superannuation schemes* run by the employees' firm or organisation deduct a certain percentage of pay directly from the gross income. (The firm also makes a contribution of a set percentage to the same pension fund.)
5   *Union dues.* These are membership fees which trade unionists pay to their particular union. In some organisations the dues are deducted from pay and the total collected remitted to the union.

Voucher   In accounts this is a written document acknowledging receipt of a sum of money and serving as proof of payment.

W

In the Telephone Alphabet W is for William

Abbreviations

w . . . . with
WE . . . . week ending
wh . . . . which
wk . . . . week
WP . . . . word processor/word processing
WPM . . . . words per minute

Wages slip (salaries and wages)   See **pay advice**.

Widow line (word processors)   The first line of a paragraph when it appears by itself at the bottom of a page.

Winchester (computers)   Name of a compact, high-speed, high-capacity hard disk, which is completely sealed in its disk drive.

Window envelopes   These envelopes have cutout panels covered with transparent material through which the address written on the letter can be read.

Word processor   See fig 59. This is a computer designed specifically to work with letters, words, paragraphs and other pieces of written information. It makes use of a computer's features, such as its versatility, speed, compactness and cost-effectiveness, for the typing, editing, storage, printing and communication of written information.

232

Word processors are equipped with VDUs so that the operator can see what he or she is actually typing on the screen. Merely by the operation of keys, text can be inserted, deleted or moved to another position. Layout

Fig 59 Word processor

adjustments are easily effected, and corrections can be made by overtyping. Documents are printed out only when they are completely correct, and they can be stored for future use. A *printer* is used with a word processor; this is a typewriter without a keyboard which can print out any 'copy', from its memory, at very high speeds.

A word-processing unit consists of the following equipment:

1   *A keyboard*   This is an electric typewriter with a normal keyboard layout but with separate function keys.

2   *A visual display unit* (VDU) which displays, immediately above the keyboard, the words being typed.

3   *A storage unit* where text can be stored on hard disks, floppy disks, magnetic tape or magnetic cards for subsequent amendment or printing.

4   *A printer* which can produce automatically at the rate of about 550 words per minute. It can accept information from the typing on the screen and from the standard information store.

The unit can be linked to a central computer so that data can be called up and then stored and processed. Also, a number of processors can be linked by telephone, allowing for automatic transfer of texts, even when the receiving processor is unattended.

Word processors are particularly useful in the following fields:

1   *Repetitive standard letters.* This covers standard correspondence of all types—sales letters in particular are important, where the information which changes from one letter to the next is usually confined to the recipient's name and address and perhaps only two or three other small details. Standard information can be stored and programmed to be input as required and word processors can construct letters from any combination of standard paragraphs.

2   *Keeping price lists, directories, mailing lists, etc up-to-date.* A word processor can do this without the necessity of retyping the whole.

3   *Typing the drafts of reports, minutes, etc.* Any amendments are effected easily on the word processor before the final copy is prepared.

Wraparound (word processors)   A feature of word processors whereby a word that cannot fit on the end of a line is automatically carried over to the next line. The operator therefore does not have to end the line manually.

X

In the Telephone Alphabet X is for X-Ray

Y

In the Telephone Alphabet Y is for Yellow

Abbreviations

yd	yard
yr	year
yrs	years, yours

Yearly plan (National Savings) This is a new scheme (1984) from National Savings for regular savers. Monthly payments (in multiples of £5, with a minimum of £20 and a maximum of £100) can be made for as little as one year, and they can continue for further years if required. It is an easy way of building up a lump sum for a major purchase or retirement, and offers guaranteed returns on the investment with tax-free interest.

Under Yearly Plan the contributor makes monthly payments for one year, all payments being made by standing order. At the end of that year he will receive a Yearly Plan certificate showing the total value of the monthly payments, including the interest earned in that year. This Certificate will then earn compound interest every month for the next four years, and can be left in the scheme to earn further interest.

Yellow pages (reference books) This is a classified business directory, which is complementary to the local telephone directory. It lists telephone subscribers in the relevant area according to trade or profession.

Z

Zero-rated (transactions)   Zero-rated goods are those on which the purchaser pays no value added tax (VAT).